NAUTICAL
TRAINING
SHIPS

An Illustrated History

NAUTICAL TRAINING SHIPS

An Illustrated History

PHIL CARRADICE

AMBERLEY

First published 2009

Amberley Publishing Plc
Cirencester Road, Chalford,
Stroud, Gloucestershire, GL6 8PE

www.amberley-books.com

Copyright © Phil Carradice 2009

The right of Phil Carradice to be identified as the Author
of this work has been asserted in accordance with the
Copyrights, Designs and Patents Act 1988.

ISBN 978 1 84868 696 0

British Library Cataloguing in Publication Data.
A catalogue record for this book is available from the
British Library.

Typeset in 10pt on 12pt Sabon.
Typesetting and Origination by FONTHILLMEDIA.
Printed in the UK.

Contents

CHAPTER ONE
Abandon Ship

It was just a few minutes short of three o' clock on Sunday afternoon, 20 January 1918. As usual, a group of officers and a few of the more experienced trainees were loitering on the main deck of the Marine Society Training Ship, *Warspite*, enjoying the luxury of a lazy Sabbath Day, watching the wind pull the tops off tiny wavelets along the river's edge.

The *Warspite* had lain at Greenhithe off the Kent shore of the Thames for many years, training needy boys for careers in the Merchant and, occasionally, Royal Navies and the officers knew both the river and their ship very well indeed. All was quiet and calm, as it should be on a Sunday afternoon.

Most of the officers chatted easily to each other, happily replete after a Sunday dinner – always dinner, never lunch – of roast beef and potatoes, but one of them was reading the newspaper as he strolled along the deck. The paper was carefully folded to stop it flapping like a loose sail in the wind, for although the day was calm there was always something of a breeze out there, a few hundred yards off shore. The war news was low-key, the officer noted. In France there was little happening, the opposing armies seeming to have settled down for the winter. German U-boats, however, were still sinking merchantmen in the Western Approaches. Gravely, the officer shook his head at the thought of sailors, many of them just boys like the ones he was training on the *Warspite*, losing their lives in the cold Atlantic waters.

Then, almost instinctively, the officer realised something was wrong. He lowered his paper, paused in his pacing and sniffed at the air. Smoke! The man dived for the warning bell. In an instant the alarm was given and, in a mad rush, boys, instructors and officers all raced to their assigned positions. Smoke meant fire and fire on any wooden warship spelled potential disaster.

Fire hoses were quickly run out, manned by officers and boys, and water began to be played into the smoke. Meanwhile, messengers were dispatched to call in those officials who were ashore for the day or on leave in Greenhithe and Stone. It was obvious that every hand would be needed if the ship were to be saved, but almost from the beginning it was clearly an impossible task.

At one stage smoke and flames cut off the crew of pump number one, situated on the main deck. They were lucky and were able to escape through the bakehouse port by means of a rope lowered down the ship's side. On board the battle continued, but within an hour the decks of the *Warspite* were filled with dense, suffocating smoke. A fire tug and a party from the nearby Shaftesbury Society training ship, *Arethusa*, arrived to help but it was no use, the fire had gained too great a hold. Everyone was exhausted by the effort of trying to quench the flames and, finally, rather than risk loss of life, Capt Supdt A. G. F. Hill was forced to call, 'Abandon Ship!' The bugle call was made at about 5.15 p.m. and all 250 boys, and their officers, quickly left the ship.

During the evening several parties of volunteers went back to the *Warspite* to fight the blaze once more while the steam hoses from the attendant tug continued to pour water into the inferno. The fire roared unabated. At 11 p.m. the main mast fell, the foremast following shortly afterwards. Just after two o' clock in the morning *Warspite* sank at her moorings. Her upper decks were, however, above the water and continued to burn until 5 a.m.

On 23 January 1918, at Gravesend Magistrates Court, three boys – Ernest Cecil Adams (14), Frederick George Blogg (15) and John Wesley Gurr (14) – were charged with setting fire to the *Warspite*. They admitted the offence, Blogg stating that he and his friends had been planning the attack since before Christmas. Adams declared that he had been asked by the other boys to go with them to the ship's hold where he saw a 'heap of wood and canvas'. Blogg ignited the pile with matches and the three boys ran out, leaving a lighted lamp behind them. This fanned the flames even further.

The three boys later appeared at the Kent Assizes where they defended themselves with allegations of excessive brutality by the ship's officers, including over-use of the cane, and claims of the existence of a dungeon situated in the forepeak. Capt Hill strenuously denied the charges, quoting records to show that in the previous fifteen months only twenty-five canings had taken place. Nevertheless, it was clear that something was amiss on the ship and that at least half of the boys had some knowledge of the plan – one of the reasons the Kent police were able to identify the arsonists with such ease. In the event, it was an open-and-shut case and the boys were each sentenced to three years in a reformatory school.[1]

The arson and sinking of the *Warspite* marked the beginning of the end to a system of nautical training that had, for many years, provided the Royal and Merchant Navies with thousands of sailors, officers and deck-hands alike – in other words, the placing of boys on old, wooden warships moored around the coast of Britain where they could be schooled in their chosen profession. The disaster did not spell the end for nautical training; indeed, it did not spell the immediate end to wooden-wall training either. Like all long-established systems, it took time to implement change and vessels like the *Conway*, *Worcester* and *Arethusa* were still in use in the 1950s. However, 1918 was the high-water mark of the system and from then onwards, in the minds of educationalists, naval planners and administrators, the use of old, wooden ships as schools and training establishments began to acquire very limited value.

There had been a degree of disquiet about the training ships for many years. Conditions on board were too cramped, too squalid, reformers had proclaimed. Disease and all sorts of unhealthy practices were rife, they said. Bullying was

A print taken from *The Illustrated London News*, 29 June 1867, showing Marine Society boys at gun drill on the training ship *Warspite*.

The second *Warspite*, destroyed by fire on Sunday 20 January 1918, as she lay at her moorings off Greenhithe.

easy, it was claimed, on the dark decks of a nineteenth-century frigate where the nefarious activities of the less humane trainees were safe from the prying eyes of authority and from almost any form of external scrutiny.

Moored in busy estuaries and rivers, there was also the perpetual risk of collision. After all, the training ships were immobile and could hardly get out of the way of oncoming vessels. In August 1863, for example, the Russian, armoured battery ship, *Pervenetz*, ran into the *Warspite*, gouging a huge hole out of her hull. Only the slow speed of the Russian ship, bound down-river for sea trials, had prevented more serious damage.[2] The wooden walls were hardy vessels, however, and sometimes the damage was all the other way. A trainee on the *Conway* later recalled that 'a small schooner ran into us one night and did herself considerable damage, leaving her main-truck in one of our cutters'.[3]

By the latter stages of the First World War, of course, the very nature of seafaring was changing. No longer did sailing ships rule the waves, although there were still plenty of them about. In 1865, the heyday of the wooden training ships, only a sixth of Britain's shipping was powered by steam, but the repeal of the Navigation Acts sixteen years earlier – removing the edict that British goods could only be carried on British ships – had already created fierce competition between Britain's merchant fleet and those of her continental and, indeed, transatlantic rivals. Britain needed a modern, fast and efficient Mercantile Marine in order to compete effectively with other nations who viewed with envious eyes her privileged position as the foremost commercial and trading country in the world.

Change did not come quickly. There were too many hidebound old ship owners around, men who saw no future in metal ships driven by steam power. It was a fad, they thought, fine for coastal trading but not on the big Atlantic and Pacific routes. No, it would never catch on. The Royal Navy was not much better. The men in charge at the Admiralty were rooted in the Nelsonian tradition, many of them having fought at Trafalgar, the battle that had effectively handed Britain control of the seas. Like their Merchant Navy counterparts, they strongly resisted the advance of steam power. It was not until 1860 that the *Warrior*, Britain's first armour clad vessel, was launched, but then, as the cult of empire began to really take hold, it became increasingly obvious that things would have to change.

In order to meet the demand for ships and more ships, by the end of the 1860s the British shipbuilding industry was producing over 300,000 new tons each year and, as the effect of new technology began to bite, most of those new vessels were made out of iron and were powered by steam.[4] By the beginning of the twentieth century, then, steam power was clearly the order of the day and the shipping companies needed youngsters who knew the intricacies of boilers, connecting rods, flanges and electrical machinery. Learning to climb masts and coil ropes was all very well but modern sailors needed more, and the old, wooden training ships were not really the place to give it to them.

However, the greatest drawback of all, as far as the wooden training ships were concerned, was the risk of fire. Including the *Warspite*, no fewer than seven training ships foundered at their moorings over the years, burned to the water-line

One of the few training ship fires caught on camera – the destruction of the *Wellesley* on 11 March 1914.

Boys in their hammocks on board a training ship. Such comfort was pure luxury for many boys who were often more used to sleeping rough on the streets.

either by accident or by arson. Indeed, the 1918 fire on board the *Warspite* was the second such disaster to befall the Marine Society, and only four years before the *Warspite* sinking the Industrial School Ship *Wellesley*, then lying at North Shields, was also destroyed by fire. The establishment had since 'come ashore' and appeared to be prospering reasonably well. So, the writing was on the wall long before 1918; the '*Warspite*' fire was, quite simply, the last straw.

No new training ships were established after 1918, although several of the existing vessels did manage to acquire steel-hulled cruisers as replacements for their wooden walls. These cruisers had become obsolete and un-needed in the post-war period, but it was only after much discussion and debate that they were given, loaned or presented by the Admiralty to the various bodies that ran the training ships. Among the schools to benefit were the *Indefatigable* on the Mersey and, as a replacement for the burned out wooden wall, the *Warspite* at Greenhithe.

From this point on, however, any new training establishments that were created – such as the J. A. Gibbs Home in Penarth and the Prince of Wales Sea Training School in Limehouse – were land-based, albeit equipped with rowing boats and sailing craft to give practical experience at sea or, at least, on the rivers and estuaries where the schools were based. Despite this they were all, most decidedly, rooted to the land. The value of the training was not yet in doubt, just the means of delivering it, and incarcerating boys on old hulks, with all the drawbacks such a process involved, was clearly a thing of the past.

The sole exception was the TS *Vindicatrix*, which in 1939, with war clouds gathering once more above Europe, was commissioned as the National Sea Training School and moored at Sharpness on the Severn. She had previously been owned by the Shipping Federation and kept in West India Dock, being used partly as a sailor's hostel and partly as a training ship that took seamen to upgrade their various certificates. She was very different from most of the schools, being designed to train youths, not boys, and her trainees, having made a conscious decision to enrol, knew exactly what they had let themselves in for.

Several training ships closed in the years immediately after 1918, their management committees finding that it was just too expensive, not to mention dangerous, to continue operations on board leaking, old wooden walls that would only become even more expensive as the years went on. The *Clio* and the *Empress* discharged their last trainees in 1919 and 1923 respectively, the *Mars* in 1929. Those that survived were the ones that had either already moved ashore or had created extensive shore establishments alongside their ships.

Although, in some cases, the use of training ships lingered on for several years after the First World War, the great days were clearly over. Memories remained, of course, along with a romantic and stubborn notion of the glory days of sail. Those memories hid the fact that seafaring in the days of sailing ships was hard, back-breaking work. The training was just as hard, particularly for boys – some as young as ten or twelve – who were often badly nourished, with poor physical development, and who, when they first arrived at their training ship, had little or no idea about what awaited them.

Various types of training ships and schools existed over the years. Some, like the *Warspite* and the Shaftesbury Society's *Arethusa*, were voluntary establishments where children of the needy poor could find a chance to climb out of the poverty trap. Others, like the reformatory school ships, *Akbar* and *Clarence*, or the Industrial School Ships, *Formidable* and *Wellesley*, were specifically designed for delinquent or semi-delinquent boys sent there by the courts. Then there were the officer training ships, *Conway* and *Worcester*, which were very much a cut above their less privileged counterparts. There were even ocean-going training ships run by companies such as Devitt & Moore. In addition, of course, there were a host of land-based schools, places like Pangbourne College, the Gravesend Sea Training School and the Prince of Wales School in Dover.

For a brief period of perhaps a hundred years, a web of nautical training establishments had spread across the country. Some of the schools had histories that stretched back two or even three centuries, although the system – if system it was – only reached its zenith in the late Victorian period. It was never a formal structure with unified aims and objectives, and nobody ever sat at its head, planning its development and progress. Yet it was real, it was alive, and in many cases it was remarkably effective.

The training of boys and young men for careers at sea is a process that has now largely disappeared. The Royal Navy still recruits and trains its officers and ratings but, with the demise of Britain's Merchant Marine, the romance of the sea has gone. There are clearly easier ways of earning a living. The stories remain, however, and the images of tall ships rounding the Horn, of dockside taverns full of returning matelots, and of sailors with girls in every port are lasting ones. So too are the stories and the histories of the training establishments that got them there in the first place, and to fully understand and appreciate those histories we need to go back to the very beginnings of the system.

CHAPTER TWO
Founding a System

In a speech at Glasgow in January 1912, Winston Spencer Churchill, then First Lord of the Admiralty, gave a clear indication of the government's view about Britain's maritime heritage and of its significance to the country. As far as the British nation was concerned, Churchill felt that 'this island has never been and never will be lacking in trained and hardy mariners bred from their boyhood up in the service of the sea'.[5] In that simple but succinct sentence the First Lord summed up the attitude of the British people in the immediately post-Victorian period. As an island nation, the sea had always played a vitally important part in Britain's history, providing her not only with the means to trade (and thereby become rich beyond all belief) but also with a way of keeping the people of the country fed. Perhaps even more importantly, the sea had been, and was to continue to be, a crucial element in the country's survival. Then, as now, stories of the press-gang and of battling East Indiamen, of Drake's Drum and Elizabethan buccaneers remained part of British folklore. When Britain was still a major power and ruling the greatest empire the world had ever seen, the romance of the sea and of ships kept small boys happy and contented and often fuelled a desire to experience life at sea first hand.

It is, therefore, surprising to learn that the concept of training sailors in their chosen profession is a relatively recent one. Equally as surprising, certainly for those who know something of the training hulks that proliferated around the coast from the middle years of the nineteenth century, the origins of formal nautical training in this country are to be found not on board ship but in land-based establishments, such as the Greencoat Collegiate and Christ's Hospital Schools.

The need for instruction in navigation for seamen had been identified by the writer Richard Hakluyt in the late sixteenth century. Hakluyt advocated the founding of a school of navigation similar to the one Spain had established at Seville.[6] Little was done about his suggestion, however, and for some time the only training that was given to seamen remained ad hoc, being picked up 'on the job' by officers and sailors alike. You joined a ship and learned your trade – there was no other way.

As the Elizabethan and Stuart ages progressed, however, the need for a strong and efficient navy became increasingly obvious. Realising that it was not always enough to rely on innate ability and the guiding hand of God, British politicians and entrepreneurs looked enviously at the successes of Dutch and Spanish mariners and Hakluyt's suggestions began to take on a new lease of life.

This was the age of great geographical and scientific discovery with men pushing at the boundaries of knowledge, eager to find out how the world worked. Astronomy, medicine and statistical analysis were all studied with a new and deep-rooted diligence. And in particular there was a sudden interest in mathematics and navigation.

Consequently, in 1672, Sir William Boreman founded the Greencoat Collegiate School on the north side of what is now Greenwich High Road. It was the first navigation school for boys in England, possibly even the world. The main thrust of the curriculum was in the area of mathematical study; able students following courses in trigonometry, algebra and other subjects relating to nautical navigation.

Compulsory education in Britain did not arrive until John Forster's Education Act of 1870 and schools such as the Greencoat Collegiate were entirely voluntary affairs. In order to qualify for admission, boys – of whom there were, initially, just twenty – had to have been born in Greenwich and be the sons of seamen, watermen or fishermen. Fees were in the region of ten shillings per quarter. It was a tenuous beginning and the establishment did not have a substantial life, but the Greencoat Collegiate School pre-dated the next and more substantial navigational school by just one year.

In 1673, Charles II established a school of navigation at Christ's Hospital School. The hospital had been in existence for many years, having been founded by Edward IV in 1553 in order to care for 'the worthy poor' of London. However, the later idea of creating a sea school within the establishment was the brainchild of Sir Robert Clayton, a wealthy benefactor to the hospital in the period immediately following the Fire of London in 1666.

Samuel Pepys, Secretary of the Admiralty, was instrumental in taking Clayton's suggestion to James, Duke of York, the brother of King Charles. James later became a disastrous and hugely unpopular king, but as Lord High Admiral he was considered both a brave general and a skilled administrator. His influence was considerable and, as a result of pressure from him and from Pepys, on 19 August 1673, Letters of Patent from Charles II allowed for 'the maintenance of forty boys . . . who having attained to competence in the Grammar and Common Arithmetic . . . may be fit to be further educated in a Mathematical School and there taught and instructed in the Art of Navigation.'[7]

The expense of founding and maintaining the Mathematical School, as the sea training school was known, was met by a grant of £1,000 from the Exchequer, an award that was given annually for the first seven years. After a course of studies, at the age of sixteen – earlier if the Master of Trinity House saw fit – boys would be bound as apprentices to a sea captain for a period of seven years. The first batch

The myth . . .

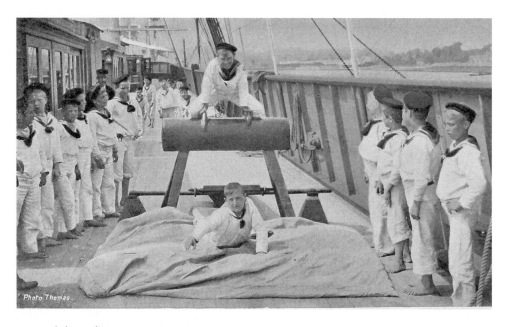

. . . and the reality.

of Bluecoat Boys, the name given to Christ's Hospital School boys because of their uniform jackets, was ready for sea by 1675, but war with Holland had ended in February the previous year and the Royal Navy had returned to a peacetime footing. There were quite simply no places on Royal Navy ships. However, thanks to the intervention of Samuel Pepys, who managed to provide a Crown Grant of just over £370, the first graduates of the Mathematical School were found berths in the Merchant Navy. The original Letters Patent from the King had made this a secondary destination for graduating boys but the economic situation being what it was there was simply no alternative.

The Dutch Wars continued, on and off, throughout the reign of Charles II and in future years the situation regarding recruitment was better. Many of the Mathematical School boys, known throughout the armed services as King's Letter Boys – because of the Letters Patent from King Charles – were offered places on Royal Navy ships.

However, the early years of the school were not always very satisfactory. One of the first teachers, Samuel Newton, was downright incompetent. Another, James Hodgson, was absent-minded. As a result, pupils were often lawless and out of control. Proper discipline was only finally exerted in 1775 when William Wales, an explorer and ex-colleague of Captain Cook, was appointed to run the school.

The boys of the Mathematical – or Nautical – School might have been delinquent, roaming the quadrangles in gangs and terrorising the other pupils with a harsh brutality that was reminiscent of the rampaging Turks, but even under men like Newton and Hodgson the quality of the training and instruction was high. When

Bluecoat Boys drilling in the playground of Christ's Hospital School, an early print from *The Illustrated Times*, 25 September 1858.

The imposing façade of the Royal Hospital School, Greenwich, seen here from the river.

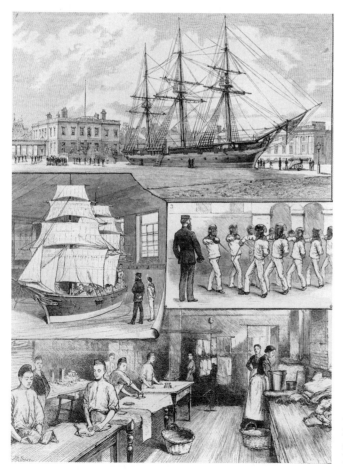

Left: A composite print, from *The Graphic*, 1875, showing various aspects of life at the school.

Above: The third and final *Fame*. Boys man the yards for the photographer.

Right: One of many small 'seamen crammers', this card and calendar for the year 1911 was produced by Cardiff Nautical Academy, an establishment long closed and long forgotten.

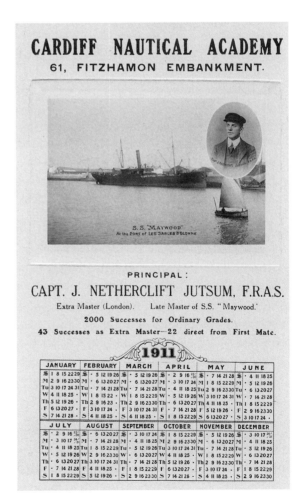

Peter the Great, Czar of Russia, visited in 1698 he was so impressed by what he saw that he decided to found his own Mathematics and Navigational School in St Petersburg. Two Bluecoat Boys, Stephen Gwyn and Richard Grice, were appointed to assist in the running of the Russian school.

William Wales was an undoubted tyrant but he was well respected and even liked by his charges. His guiding principle was that the boys should be properly prepared for their future careers and that meant facing up to harsh and brutal living conditions. No less a person than the essayist and writer Charles Lamb, himself a student at Christ's Hospital, though not a member of the Mathematical School, between 1782 and 1789 wrote about Wales: 'All his systems were adapted to fit them for the rough element which they were destined to encounter. Frequent and severe punishments, which were expected to be borne with more than Spartan fortitude, came to be considered less as inflictions of disgrace than as trials of obstinate endurance.'[8]

The boys in the Mathematical School formed something of a society apart from the other students. Distinguished by a metal badge on the left shoulder of their already distinctive blue uniforms, most of them were older than the other lads. Being different from the rest of the school, they were almost deified by their tales of escaping from the masters, the beatings they received on their return and the way they were locked in prison cells as punishment! They were, in Lamb's phrase, 'absolute nuisances to the rest of the school. Hardy, brutal, and often wicked, they were the most graceless lump in the whole mass; older and bigger than the other boys (for, by the system of their education, they were kept longer at school by two or three years) . . . they were a constant terror to the younger part of the school.'[9] Despite their bullying and arrogance, the boys were strong, and excellent athletes. The fame of the school on the sporting field soon spread far and wide.

It is with another famous land-based establishment, however, that sea training in Britain really took off. This was the Royal Hospital School at Greenwich, the buildings occupied by the school now being more easily identifiable as the home of the National Maritime Museum.

Once again the initial impetus came from Charles II and his brother James, but this time their idea had little to do with nautical training or with children. The Royal Hospital was intended to be a safe haven for aged and infirm sailors, men who had fallen on hard times once their service days were over. It was to be a place where they could retire and live out their last days watching the ships sail down the River Thames, a provision that was to be similar to the one created for retired soldiers at Chelsea. The idea was still being discussed when Charles died and it was shelved during the short and embittered reign of his Catholic brother, James. It was only when William of Orange and his wife Mary came to the throne after the Bloodless Revolution of 1688 that the idea was given a new lease of life.

After the Battle of La Hogue in 1692, when the French fleet was utterly destroyed, it was decided, as a thanksgiving for victory, to add to the idea of a home or hospital for pensioners. Care and education would now also be offered to the children of seamen who had been killed or injured in the service of their country.[10]

Henry VIII's old Palace of Placentia at Greenwich was chosen as a site and Sir Christopher Wren agreed to design the new buildings. After the death of Queen Mary, perhaps as a distraction, William threw all of his energy into the project. As it was, Wren's work was not completed until 1704, two years after William's death, and the first forty-two boys did not arrive until January 1705.

During the early years there was no school, just a set of accommodation buildings that provided the boys with a roof over their heads and very little more. Education or training for the careers they had chosen had to be found elsewhere. Various schools were attached to the Royal Hospital, the original one being closely connected with the nearby Royal Observatory. Charles II had appointed John Flamstead as his 'Astronomical Observer' in 1675 and to supplement his meagre salary of just £100 a year he decided to take in pupils. Several of these came from Christ's Hospital, most from the Royal Hospital School, while one of his early students was Thomas Weston who went on to found Weston's Academy, another school that had strong connections with the Royal Hospital in its early days. Several more educational and navigational emporiums in the Greenwich area provided assistance, each of them offering their services with greater or lesser degrees of efficiency.

The first Greenwich Hospital School regulations relating specifically to nautical training date from 1719 when it was stated that boys were 'to be put out as Apprentices to Masters of Ships and Substantial Commanders, for better improvements of their talents, and becoming Able Seamen and good Artists'.[11] Good artists were essential on board ship in these pre-photography days. Sailors needed to be able to draw charts and maps as well as often being required to reproduce views of newly discovered lands. A good sailor who was also adept with pen and brushes could, literally, dictate the conditions of his berth.

In 1694 King William had granted £2,000 a year towards the upkeep of the hospital, and other wealthy benefactors also gave voluntary endowments. However, the chief income of the school came from the unique concept of 'seamen's sixpences'. From 1695 onwards sixpence was deducted each month from the wages of all mariners, Royal and Merchant Navies alike. There was to be no debate or argument, the money was collected at source and passed on to the Hospital School.

As far as the Royal Navy was concerned this procedure continued until 1829. In its last year alone the Royal Navy levy raised the enormous sum of £21,000. Merchant seamen's sixpences continued to be deducted until December 1834 when the system was finally ended by Act of Parliament and replaced by a government grant of £20,000. Over the years the Merchant seamen's donations had been even more profitable, regularly bringing the school an annual income of over £22,000.

In 1728 there were just thirty boys at the school. By 1731 that number had risen to sixty, and by 1744 there were over 100 pupils on roll. Regulations governing admission were altered in 1734 to include not just the sons of sailors who had died but also the sons of pensioners at the Hospital, the sons of sailors who were past reasonable labour and the sons of sailors who had five or more children and were the objects of charity. However, it was some time before anyone considered providing a school within the confines of the Hospital. A new education building was eventually designed to hold 200 boys and was opened late in 1783.

Conditions were undoubtedly harsh at the school. Between 1750 and 1850, tea and cocoa were unheard of luxuries, although each boy was allowed a quart of beer daily! Plumb pudding once a week, butter three times a week, and beef once a week were the highlights of the dietary arrangements. Boys rose at 6 a.m. – an hour earlier in the summer – and began working at domestic tasks. Breakfast was taken at 8 a.m., dinner at 1 and supper was at 6 p.m. Lights out came at 9 p.m.

In between, the day was taken up with education and nautical instruction. Clean shirts were issued once a week, while new pillowcases were given out only once a month. Corporal punishment was common, beatings being inflicted by a naval drummer. One of his other duties was to drum students to meals, lessons and, eventually, to bed.[12]

Boys, at this stage, were all 'charity cases'. Poverty, whilst not having quite the same stigma as delinquency, was still not to be taken lightly. The general attitude was that people were poor because they did not work hard enough and therefore had to be made to appreciate the benefits of honest toil. The rigorous regime of places like the Royal Hospital School was deliberately created as part of the improving process.

The early history of the school is full of exciting and momentous events. On the night of 10 October 1806 body-snatchers were disturbed as they tried to dig up the remains of pensioners who had died at the hospital. The boys gave chase and three exhumed bodies were left lying on the ground as the grave-robbers fled. For a brief period girls had been admitted to the school, over 200 of them being trained for domestic service in the houses of the well-to-do. As an experiment, however, it was not a success as the boys and girls were 'constantly devising plans for surreptitious communications and clandestine intercourse'.[13] After a detailed enquiry it was decided to remove the girls from the school. By 1841, they were all gone and the experiment was not repeated.

In 1843, in order to give boys practical experience of work aloft, a ship was built in the grounds. Known as the *Fame*, she was constructed at Chatham Dockyard, dismantled and brought to Greenwich where she was rebuilt inside a walled enclosure that had once been the girls' playground. *Fame* had full rigging and ten gun ports on each quarter. Stored below decks were cutlasses, pikes and staves, designed to give boys the full experience of life on board ship. Given the fact that the *Fame* was sited on dry land, there is a degree of irony in the fact that the vessel soon began to rot and had to be replaced with a new ship. This second *Fame* also rotted away, possibly due to rising damp, and so a third vessel of the same name was built in 1872.

By the middle years of the nineteenth century, then, the Greencoat Collegiate School, Christ's Hospital School and the Royal Hospital School at Greenwich had all provided a clear and consistent thrust for nautical training. They were the premier training establishments but they were not alone.

Acts of Parliament in 1850 and 1854 established the framework to create Schools of Navigation across the country, with the help of grants from the Science and Art Department, forerunner of the Department of Education. By 1862, there were seventeen such schools in existence in fifteen different ports. Trinity House, the General Lighthouse and Pilotage Authority, was also, until 1854, a charitable organisation that could offer help for the relief of mariners and their families. It had founded several schools, including one at Newcastle in 1712. The intention of this school was 'to educate, free of charge, the children of the poor brethren in writing and mathematics. Sometime after 1716 the curriculum was extended to include navigation'.[14]

The Newcastle School, like all Trinity House Schools, did not confine itself just to teaching boys. It also taught the rudiments of navigation to men. Unfortunately, at Newcastle men and boys were apparently taught in the same room, something that did not please the Board of Trade Inspector when he came to view the establishment. It was, he felt, too demanding a task with the teacher's attention divided between two disparate groups whose needs and abilities were markedly different.[15]

Other Navigational Schools of note were the Hull Trinity House School and the Sunderland Board of Trade School. At Hull there was a lower and upper department

Boys gather to watch a boxing match on the deck of the Marine Society ship *Warspite* – the boys in front, however, seem more interested in the camera than the action in the makeshift ring.

as well as the use of assistant masters, a system that allowed boys and men to be taught separately. A common curriculum applied to all three schools, covering topics such as use of the sextant, chart drawing, meteorology, trigonometry and the code of signals. From 1857 onwards the school at Sunderland even included the study of steam engines in its curriculum.[16]

The problem with such schools was that, while the calibre of the students was invariably high, very few of them wished to make seafaring their profession. The boys, in particular, were making use of the system to access schooling that was otherwise unavailable to people with limited means. After the passing of the 1870 Education Act, legislation that made education both compulsory and readily available, they had no need of such establishments and the schools declined and inevitably closed in the last few decades of the century.

Where the students of Trinity House and independent schools did wish to make a career at sea – and these were usually young men rather than boys – the results were often spectacular. The redoubtable Sarah Jane Rees, for example, ran a Navigation School at Llangrannog on the coast of Wales during the second half of the nineteenth century, helping whole generations of local seafarers gain their Board of Trade Certificates. Most large ports had their 'seamen crammers', small establishments where ex-captains helped young sailors, who had already had experience of life at sea, gain their much-needed qualifications.

For boys, however, the provision was much more patchy. As late as 1861 the Newcastle Commission into the State of Popular Education was making it clear that there was a great weakness in the provision of nautical and navigational training for boys in many of the main maritime areas of the country. Asst Commissioner John Middleton Hare, whose particular responsibility included the towns of Hull, Yarmouth and Ipswich, where seafaring was one of the main forms of employment, commented that 'navigation is not taught in any of the public day schools . . . At Ipswich there is no navigation school of any kind'.[17] Such provision as did exist can hardly be classified as nautical training in the truest sense. Navigation and mathematics were the main aim of the Trinity House and Board of Trade Schools. But there were exceptions. At the Sunderland Board of Trade School boys were given practical experience of using ropes and working the rigging on board a sailing vessel in the harbour. At the nearby Sunderland Orphan Asylum a model ship in the grounds gave some practical help to any poor boy who might be interested in going to sea. It did not last. Governors at the orphanage ended this practice by declaring that the model could no longer be used, as boys clambering over the decks and rigging would only shorten its life!

For the majority of poor and needy youngsters, if they could not gain admission to the Royal Hospital School at Greenwich the main – indeed, for many years, the only – provision was the famous Marine Society.

Founded on 25 June 1756 by the merchant Jonas Hanway, by Sir John Fielding (brother of the novelist, Henry) and by the Duke of Bolton, the Marine Society can justifiably claim to be the oldest marine charity in the world. In 1756, the Seven Years War had just broken out and there was an urgent need for sailors to man the King's ships. Following an open meeting at the King's Arms Tavern in Cornhill, members of the society simply gathered together a number of poor and destitute boys, clothed them, thanks to the contents of the Duke's wallet, and sent them off to serve their country on HMS *Barfleur*. Press-ganging and philanthropy were thus neatly combined in an exercise that pleased both government and, in the main, the boys themselves.

By the end of the Seven Years War 5,451 men and 5,174 boys had been recruited for the navy. At the headquarters of the Marine Society above the Royal Exchange, the would-be sailors were cleaned up, kitted out and sent off to their ships armed simply with a copy of Hanway's *Christian Knowledge Made Easy* clutched to their chests. It sounds horrific but so too was the alternative for so many of the society's recruits – slow starvation on the streets of London or a descent into crime which could spell transportation or even the gallows.

The end of the war did not signal the end of the Marine Society's activities. By 1815, a further 31,000 boys had entered the Royal Navy thanks to its efforts and even after the end of the Napoleonic Wars tens of thousands of men and boys were sent to sea, mostly on the ships of the East India Company and on the fishing fleets of the east coast.[18]

In 1773, Jonas Hanway had presented the Marine Society with a detailed proposal for a nationwide system of Free Naval Schools. It was a far-sighted concept but the society could not afford to back such a grand scheme. However, in 1786 it did manage to obtain the use of a 350-ton sloop, the *Beatty*, and on 13 September the same year began offering pre-sea training or instruction on board the old ship. Moored off Deptford, the *Beatty* was soon renamed 'The Marine Society' and was the first ship-based training establishment in the world. The first intake consisted of just thirty boys in the charge of a superintendent, mate, bosun and cook. From that point on almost 200 boys were in training with the Marine Society every year until the outbreak of the Second World War in 1939.

The original vessel, *Beatty*, even before she was loaned to the Marine Society, was old and leaking like a sieve. In 1779, the Admiralty, recognising the value of pre-sea training, agreed to replace the ship with HMS *Thorn*, thus beginning the system of loaning out old, wooden warships, a system of which the society and many other organisations were to make full use in the years ahead.

Over the next hundred or so years the Marine Society had the use of many different vessels. The *Thorn* was eventually replaced by the *Solebay*, and she, in turn, was succeeded by the *Iphigenia* in 1833. The *Venus* arrived in 1848 and the first of the famous *Warspites* came to the Thames in 1862.

The land-based nautical and navigational schools had effectively begun a whole system or style of training and the Marine Society, with its acquisition of the *Beatty*, had shown the way forward. The success of the Society in placing boys, in particular, into positions on board ship was remarkable, and to Victorian philanthropists it seemed as if one of the answers to the poverty trap was on hand. Practical sea training, it seemed, was best provided on board ship where the trainees could experience the life they were soon to lead first hand.

CHAPTER THREE
Reformatory School Ships

During the first half of the nineteenth century, Britain found itself in the throes of rapid industrialisation, its population desperately attempting to come to terms with an unparalleled series of social and economic changes. The speed of these changes was often terrifying as whole families abandoned the villages or hamlets where they had been established for years, decamping to the mushrooming towns of the industrial regions. London was particularly hard hit. Between 1801 and 1851 the population of the capital grew from 1,117,000 to an amazing 2,685,000. By 1861 that figure had risen again, leaping to 3,227,000.[19]

In all the industrial towns – in Birmingham and Liverpool, Bristol and Sheffield – there were desperate shortages of housing, of clean water supplies, of hospitals and schools. Discontent was rife, often flaring up into open rebellion and rioting. Outbreaks of cholera, typhoid and other infectious diseases were a common occurrence in the teeming slum tenements.

Above all, there was an unprecedented rise in the birth rate. In 1751, the number of men, women and children living in Britain was approximately six million – a hundred years later the figure was a staggering 18,000,000. In the words of the writer Jo Manton: 'Children, one of the most vulnerable social groups, showed the strain most. Many had to fend for themselves from earliest childhood, and those who could not find work or friends stole.'[20]

The British people, increasingly concerned about the thin veneer or fabric of society, could not push away or disregard the problems of the criminal classes. During the eighteenth century there had been no separate treatment of juvenile offenders who were dealt with by precisely the same means as their adult counterparts. In 1785, for example, eighteen out of the twenty-one prisoners executed in the city of London were below the age of twenty-one.[21]

Faced by harsh or even cruel and unjust laws, which included punishments such as whipping, branding and hanging for what would now be regarded as relatively trivial offences, many of the more enlightened citizens chose to administer their own justice – a box around the ears or a ducking in the village pond – rather than report juvenile offenders to the authorities. However, as the nineteenth century unfolded, things began to change. Imprisonment began to replace the harsher penalties such as hanging and while this was to be applauded it also made punishment a great deal more certain. Individuals were now far less likely to take matters into their own hands – 'let the law take its course' became the general attitude.

There was an immediate increase in the number of juveniles in the prison system. In 1847 alone, 1,767 youngsters were sent to prison – a staggeringly high figure. Over the previous ten years committals of young offenders had risen from 2,009 to 3,212 and young people under the age of twenty-one now regularly made up one-third of the annual penal calendar.[22] Quite clearly, the problem of juvenile crime was a serious and worrying matter.

As there was no separate prison system for juveniles, once young offenders entered the looming portals of the local bridewell they came into regular contact with hardened criminals. There they were effectively schooled at their chosen profession in what were, really, academies of crime.

By the early years of the nineteenth century transportation had become a well-used punishment. Those awaiting transportation were usually locked up on old hulks moored in the wilder reaches of the Thames, as depicted in Charles Dickens' *Great Expectations*. In 1815, the notoriously corrupt and inefficient J. H. Capper was appointed superintendent of these hulks and made no secret of the fact that his ships would cater for children as well as adults.

The hulks were overcrowded and conditions were appalling. There was little to do on board – no work or schooling – and the youngsters were left to their own devices. Discipline was lax and Capper made himself a fortune through a variety of illicit dealings. In the 1820s the *Bellerophon* at Sheerness and the *Euryalus* at Chatham were designated as hulks for children only, but the environment on board both ships was so bad that the conditions of the streets were simply being reproduced below deck. Several mutinies took place and bullying was a constant factor. Even Capper was forced to admit that the experiment had not worked and in 1842 it came to an inglorious end. However, it had shown that confinement on board ship, if organised correctly, might be one way of dealing with juvenile crime.

The 1840s and '50s saw considerable debate around the issue of juvenile crime, not least because transportation of criminals had been suspended in 1846 and finally abolished in 1852. At the forefront of discussion were the Rev. Sydney Turner and the formidable Mary Carpenter. Nobody had previously displayed such zeal and dynamism in debating the issue of young offenders as Mary Carpenter. In her book, *Reformatory Schools for the Children of the Perishing and Dangerous Classes*, she advocated the establishment of a system of reformatories purely for young offenders and those who were likely to become offenders if something was not done quickly: 'These schools will produce the desired effect of checking the progress of crime in those who have not yet subjected themselves to the grasp of the law, and of reforming those who are already convicted criminals.'[23]

There were already one or two voluntary establishments in the country, places like Sydney Turner's Royal Philanthropic Society Reformatory at Redhill, but Mary Carpenter wanted a whole range of them. She wanted children out of the prison system and she wanted them cared for, not punished. After much discussion

Left: Training on board ship had its origins in the old prison hulks and in the convict ships that once took prisoners to Australia. This view shows one of the original convict ships.

Below: The second *Akbar*, Liverpool's first reformatory school ship. She is shown here dressed overall for Queen Victoria's Jubilee in 1897.

and parliamentary lobbying in 1854 An Act for the better care and reformation of criminal offenders in Great Britain was passed. Most of the credit for this revolutionary piece of legislation has to belong to Mary Carpenter, the Act clearly indicating that she had got her way: 'Reformatory Schools for the better training of juvenile offenders . . . may be established by voluntary contributions in various parts of Great Britain, and . . . it is expedient that more extensive use should be made of such institutions.'[24]

For the first time reformatory schools became official, taking boys (and girls) under the age of sixteen years for periods of not less than two and not more than five years. One drawback of the system was that the schools were to be run by voluntary bodies. The government would certify them and inspect them but it was not yet ready to plough huge sums of money into such a new and untried system. Such a compromise was, in many ways, typical of the Victorian age where Samuel Smiles' doctrine of 'self help' still held sway. However, it was a start. Provided the organising committees could obtain their certificates from the Home Office, they could now found and run a reformatory school.

Mary Carpenter and her colleagues realised that the system was not perfect. For example, youngsters still had to serve a preliminary prison sentence of at least fourteen days before they could be transferred to a reformatory, a process that Carpenter saw as counter-productive and downright dangerous. The legislation was also not compulsory, magistrates simply being given the option of using a reformatory school rather than the traditional prison sentence. Despite Carpenter's objections, however, a plethora of schools soon sprang up right across Britain, and it was not long before they began to fill with young offenders.

The origins of reformatory schools on board ship remain unclear. No one knows where the idea came from but, as the list of reformatories grew, somebody had the notion that reformatory training along naval or nautical lines would be an excellent thing. Naval discipline, secure confinement on board ship (as on the old transportation hulks) and the fact that the Royal and Merchant Navies were constantly in need of sailors: these were the governing factors behind the creation of a system of water-borne reformatories. The bustling port of Liverpool was at the front of this new and dynamic thrust.

On Thursday 11 January 1855, a group of churchmen, ship owners and local dignitaries met in the Magistrate's Room of the Session House to form the Liverpool Juvenile Reformatory Association. They resolved to establish three reformatories on Merseyside, two for boys and one for girls. Importantly, one of the boys' schools was to be based on board ship and was to run a naval regime.

The *Akbar* had been built at Bombay in 1801, but by the middle years of the century was on quarantine duty at Liverpool. At any one time the port was temporary home for thousands of sailors from all over the world, and any of them could bring in dreaded diseases such as smallpox, cholera or even bubonic plague, hence the need for a quarantine vessel.

The Liverpool Juvenile Reformatory Association quickly set about acquiring the *Akbar*, despite its rather dilapidated condition, and spent £2,000 on making the

The Mersey boasted two reformatory ships, the *Akbar* and the *Clarence*, as well as the industrial training ship *Indefatigable* and the officer training ship *Conway*. This shot gives an indication of the views along the river at the end of the nineteenth century.

vessel shipshape. She received her certificate from the Home Office on 3 January 1856 and, within days, began to take boys on board. Moored off Rock Ferry, the first *Akbar* was replaced by the *Hero* in 1862. The committee decided to retain the original name and the *Hero*, now rechristened *Akbar*, served as a reformatory school for nearly fifty years, becoming a famous landmark on the Mersey.

The city of Liverpool was obviously a major user but magistrates were soon making referrals from places like Birkenhead, Manchester and the other industrial towns of the north-west. As long as there were vacancies the committee was happy to receive them. Several boys came from other reformatories. These were boys who, it was felt, needed harsher discipline and tighter controls than those supplied by normal reformatory schools. The Committee also received direct applications from parents who were desperate to control unruly and disruptive children.

The *Akbar* was undoubtedly well run, despite the rather truculent nature of many of the boys. The 25th Report of the Inspector of Reformatory and Industrial Schools (1882) was fulsome in its praise for the ship, as were most of the other annual inspection reports. It stated that 'as far as good order, cleanliness and suitable arrangements can affect it, she must take a foremost place amongst our training ships.'[25]

The first superintendent was Mr Edward Hambleton who was employed on a salary of £80 a year. He was assisted by a schoolmaster, a bosun, a joiner, a cook and two seamen. His wife and child were to live on board with him, the food of all three being an extra to his salary. In the event, Hambleton did not stay long and by 1857 he had been replaced by Capt Fenwick. Known as the Captain Superintendent, Fenwick was the first of the ex-naval officers who, in future, were always appointed to run the reformatory and industrial school ships.

The *Clarence*, a Catholic reformatory ship, later burned out at her moorings.

While the captain and crew were provided with smart naval outfits, complete with gold braid and gilt buttons, boys were dressed in blue trousers and Guernsey jumpers. For ceremonial occasions each of them was given a sailor's suit, complete with glazed hat. Such outfits were probably the first decent clothing that most of them had ever owned.

Parents were expected, wherever possible, to contribute to the cost of keeping their children on board. Failure to contribute even a small amount could result in a court appearance when offenders could be fined, have goods confiscated or be sent to prison. A government treasury grant of six shillings per head, per week, for every boy on board plus voluntary contributions from friends and benefactors were, however, the main means of funding the ship. The Treasury contribution remained a constant factor, even though it was never a large sum. By 1867, for example, it was still set at only seven shillings and sixpence for each boy.

The amount and quality of voluntary contributions varied greatly. Sometimes the *Akbar* was lucky to receive gifts such as two harbour cutters, donated in 1858 by the Storekeeper General. That same year one of the committee members provided the ship with a set of topgallant sails. On other occasions the captain and crew were happy to receive what little money people could spare or even the turnips and rhubarb from local gardens. The cost of running the ship was high and in 1882 the total running costs for all three Merseyside reformatories was over £8,000.

Despite being well run, conditions on board the *Akbar* were harsh and sometimes quite brutal, but the brutality needs to be put into the context of the times. The causes of juvenile crime, in the eyes of most Victorians, were complex and varied. Lack of education was one cause, the corrupting influence of the home and neighbourhood was another. Above all, they felt, there was the total lack of religious and moral values and knowledge. This last cause was felt to be highly significant.

Whilst most reformers and philanthropists were driven by Christian charity, there was also a clear belief that 'the degraded and fallen ones' should not be elevated above their social grouping and standing in life. The ability to earn an honest living was the most important purpose behind any form of intervention or training, hence the desire to train boys for careers at sea. There would always be a need for sailors, not least because of the deadly nature of the profession. To take just one year as an example, Board of Trade figures for 1861 show that almost 4,000 sailors lost their lives in the twelve-month period. That represents one in fifty six of all those who went to sea on British ships and sits very uneasily when compared to the equivalent death rate amongst miners for the same period – 1 in 350.[26]

So conditions on the *Akbar* were made deliberately hard and frugal. Nobody in a position of power wished to see a boy from a reformatory school rise to an exceptional position. Rather, he should be made to fall into the great mass of humanity who survived by hard, honest labour, depending on the sweat of their brow, not benevolence or patronage of any kind.

The punitive element of life on board the ship was clear for all to see. And the punishments imbued all aspects of the daily routine, from the regimes and curriculum to the food and clothing provided. The comments of the inspectors with regards to the clothing and food of the boys was particularly poignant. As one inspector was moved to remark: 'I do not believe that death would reap such a harvest from pneumonia if funds allowed more liberal clothing and more sustaining food.'[27]

In the eyes of many, providing any form of education for delinquent boys was a mistake. Even some of the committee members felt that, in the days before education was available for all, it was wrong to provide such a privilege for boys who had proved their lack of worth to society by their actions. So the daily routine on the *Akbar* was long and hard with the emphasis on manual labour rather than schooling.

Boys rose at 5 a.m. and lights out was at 8 p.m. During the day they scrubbed the decks with coconut husks, repaired clothing and made shoes. The sale of these shoes brought in limited industrial profit and also made some money for the boys themselves. Other tasks included shredding old rope to make oakum, building sea chests and tailoring. Limited education and sea training were provided, the training mainly consisting of learning how to launch and use small boats, how to coil and throw ropes and so on. It was pretty basic fare but the essential purpose of being on board the *Akbar* was only partly to educate a boy. The primary aim, most people felt, was for a boy to undergo the discipline which he had clearly not had up to that point in his life, discipline that would deter him from a life of crime: 'by having the inmates . . . inured to continuous labour, we can best hope to wean them from indolent and vicious habits, and inspire them with a love of

The Royal Navy's refusal to take boys with a criminal record gave the Training Ship Committees a severe headache. This carte de visite shows a *Clio* boy in full uniform – Arthur Byron, who was discharged from the Royal Navy because of a long-forgotten offence, would have worn a uniform like this. (photograph courtesy of the Stephen Rowson Collection)

honest toil, thus implanting in their minds the thought of self dependence and self respect.'[28]

Given such attitudes, it is remarkable that any of the *Akbar* boys ever managed to find berths on board ship, but they did. Returns relating to the reformatory and industrial school ships for the period 1891 to 1895 show that no fewer than 165 boys out of a total number of 258 discharges went to sea when they left their ship.[29]

Recreation on board was limited, consisting mainly of games such as draughts or bagatelle. Swimming in the Mersey was a popular pastime, particularly in the summer. The instructors were proud of the fact that most boys managed to learn to swim during their time on board but, even so, a number of drownings did occur. Sundays were invariably taken up with Bible studies and religious services.

Certified by the Home Office to take 200 boys, by March 1858 there were 158 on board. By 1876, the figure had risen to 190. It must have been a cramped, cold environment and death and injury were ever-present visitors. The minute books of the committee tell the sad tale in bare and sparse details: 'Thomas, while employed in blacking a portion of the rigging, was accidentally jerked off and thrown down from a height of 16 feet onto the deck, dying there three hours later.' And then again: 'William, while manning the working boat, slipped and was crushed between the boat and the ship side. His body was washed up on shore.'[30]

Sadly, there was little or no attempt at selection. Boys were supposed to be strong enough to withstand the rigours of life on board ship, but referrals meant

Boys from the *Clarence* pose on the mast and deck of their ship.

money for the committee – the more boys on board, the higher the treasury grant - and a boy would have to be a pretty poor specimen to be refused a place. In reality most boys were under-sized, poorly nourished and often suffering from rickets. Many were as young as ten or eleven years old and totally unsuited to such hard, exhausting training.

The *Akbar* was not the only reformatory ship on the Mersey. On 15 August 1864, the *Clarence* received her certificate from the Home Office and was moored off New Ferry. Founded and run by the Liverpool Committee of the Catholic Reformatory Association, she was the product of hard work by Father Nugent, a well-respected Liverpool priest, and by many Catholic businessmen from the city. As the name of the association suggests, the *Clarence* was intended to provide Catholic boys with naval discipline and nautical training.

The *Clarence* was an eighty-four-gun man-of-war, launched from the Welsh dockyard of Pembroke Dock in July 1827. Now at the end of her useful life, she was intended to cater for 250 boys but was rarely full. She was reasonably successful, however, in sending a high proportion of her boys to sea. In 1888, there were fifty-nine discharges – forty-one of them joined the Merchant Navy. The following year twenty-two out of thirty-six went to sea, and in 1890 the figure was thirty-one out of thirty-nine discharges. That gave a percentage figure of 70.15 per cent of all discharges taking up the sea.[31]

While the original intention had been to send boys from the reformatory ships to both the Royal and Merchant Navies, this was soon found to be impossible.

The reformatory ship *Cornwall* moored at Purfleet on the Thames.

The days of the press-gang, when anyone who could walk was a likely candidate, were long gone, and the Royal Navy, now able to be considerably more choosy, refused to accept boys with criminal records. This automatically ruled out most reformatory school boys. The Merchant Navy was not nearly so rigorous and, as a consequence, boys tended to be placed there or with the country's fishing fleets.

The intransigence of the Royal Navy is best seen in the case of Arthur Byron who was sent not to a reformatory but to the industrial ship *Clio* in April 1898. A strong, intelligent lad, his crime, such as it was, was truancy. He did well on board the *Clio* and, at the age of sixteen applied for and was accepted for training in the Royal Navy on board HMS *Lion*. A few months into his training it was discovered that, long before he went to the *Clio*, Byron had been charged with – but never convicted of – two cases of theft. He was promptly discharged from the Navy and no amount of pleading from the boy, staff from the *Clio*, or the Home Office could make the Admiralty change their mind.

As a result of the attitude of the Admiralty almost all boys on the reformatory ships were considered only for the Merchant Navy. The regime on board the *Clarence* was broadly similar to that of the *Akbar*. However, in light of the numerous troubles that beset the ship – and considering the high success rate in finding boys berths at sea – it is fair to surmise that greater thought was given to training than to control. Finding the correct balance between control and education/training was clearly difficult. The original *Clarence* suffered the ignominy of being burned to the water-line in 1884, while its replacement also suffered the same fate – but more of this later!

In 1882, the Inspector of Reformatory and Industrial Schools was commenting that, as far as the *Clarence* was concerned: 'the year has been marked by a larger

A close up view of the bow section of the *Cornwall*. Note the net below the mast to catch unwary trainees who might fall from the futtock shrouds.

measure of unruliness and insubordination than usual, several cases of absconding, and rather more insolence and rudeness than in former years.'[32]

Part of the trouble lay in the fact that by 1882 Capt Algar had retired. Algar had been in control of the *Clarence* since her early days, and much of the school's success was down to him. He was replaced by Capt Hudson who clearly needed time to settle into his new post.

A third reformatory ship, the *Cornwall*, was certificated on 5 May 1859. Moored at Purfleet on the Thames, she was the brainchild of George Chambers, a London businessman, who had watched with interest as the *Akbar* had been established on the Mersey and who soon decided that London would benefit from a similar vessel. Chambers' School Ship Society duly applied to the Admiralty for the loan of a disused wooden wall and the fifty-gun frigate, *Cornwall*, was quickly donated, on the condition that sufficient funds could be raised to equip her. In a remarkably short space of time, £2,000 was gathered together, thanks to voluntary subscriptions from the public, and a working committee was formed. In April 1859, the *Cornwall* was towed to Purfleet, which was at that time a rather isolated part of the Thames. The nearest habitation was a government powder magazine on shore.

The first captain superintendent of the *Cornwall* was Augustus Burton, ex-Royal Navy, and the first boy was admitted on 6 June 1859. By December that year there were forty-six boys on board.

Choosing the right man to run the *Cornwall* always seemed to be a tricky problem. As late as 1923, Capt Woodward was 'wished' on the committee by the Admiralty because he was so idle. The Admiralty, of course, had little or no say in the running of the ship but it did not pay to annoy or antagonise them too much; after all, it was the Admiralty that loaned the vessels in the first place. One

Boys pose on the deck of the *Cornwall*. They look like angels but according to the Schools Inspector they were some of 'the most vicious, troublesome and incorrigible lads in Great Britain.'

of the best captain superintendents was Capt Steele who, unfortunately, died in post during the First World War. As it was impossible to find a successor during a time of national crisis, his wife took over the running of the ship for a short while, taking full charge of all education and training on board.

As with the *Akbar* and *Clarence*, discipline on board the *Cornwall* was strict and the regime was almost Spartan in its severity. The diet on all the ships was basic but filling, as it needed to be on the cold, windswept Thames and Mersey. 'Recently improved dietaries' for the *Cornwall* from 1906 show that the staple food of the boys was Irish stew, potatoes and bread. Butter was a rarity, as were eggs, fruit and green vegetables. Cocoa and milk, however, do seem to have been readily available.

By 1868 over 200 boys were in training on board the *Cornwall* and the ship, although certificated for 250, was nearing capacity. Consequently, when the committee heard that the *Wellesley*, then a receiving ship for the Royal Navy on the Tyne, was about to be broken up, they approached the Admiralty with a view to obtaining her. The new ship arrived at Purfleet and took the name *Cornwall* on 18 June 1868. Unlike so many of the vessels that served as reformatory and industrial schools, this new ship, valued at £4,217, came fully equipped with masts, rigging and stores.

There is no doubt that the three reformatory ships provided a cutting edge in the Victorian fight against juvenile crime. They may not always have been totally successful in placing boys in careers at sea but this was only ever one part of their purpose. With an exactitude that shows the Victorian love of statistics and figures, Henry Rogers, Inspector of Reformatory and Industrial Schools, commented on 12 March 1891: 'The Reformatory Ships deal with some of the most vicious, troublesome and incorrigible lads in Great Britain. These ships were founded for the purpose of getting such lads out of mischief and off the streets. This is affected to a considerable extent. About 60% of the Reformatory boys go to sea . . . and 71.66 per cent of these do well. Only a small percentage are reconvicted. This is as much as can be fairly expected.'[33]

Each of the reformatory ships, like the land-based schools, was inspected by the Home Office on an annual basis, the responsibility falling to the Inspector of Reformatory and Industrial Schools. The first inspection took place in 1857 when only the *Akbar* was working, the ship being subjected to scrutiny on 30 April. It was noted that there were 150 boys on board and that the ship was 'one of the most effective Reformatories . . . The ship is in admirable order, and the boys cheerful, active and obedient; their knowledge of Scriptures and general things is very satisfactory'.[34] Interestingly, no comment is made anywhere in the report about the nautical training the boys received. The ship had cost £2,192 10s 0d to maintain for the year and industrial profits had amounted to only £91 11s 0d.

A year later the Second Report of the Inspector of Reformatory and Industrial Schools was reporting that there had been six discharges from the *Akbar* in 1856 and twenty-four in 1857. Of these only one had been reconvicted, fourteen were known to be doing well and four were dead. The whereabouts of eleven of the boys was unknown.[35] The Inspector's Report for 1889 covered the *Clarence* and *Cornwall* as well as the *Akbar*. With regard to the *Cornwall*, it was clear that nautical training was limited to one class for sail making and another where boys were taught to work with wire rope for rigging. The report stated that 'one boy has been taken before the Magistrates for assault, and had six weeks hard labour. There have been three cases of absconding'.[36]

The *Clarence* was inspected in March that year. Nautical training appeared to be well covered with boys being taught how to make and shorten sail. They were all able to send down yards from above while the various appliances used for training, such as boats, compasses and sextants, were felt to be of the highest quality. Particular praise was given to the steering gear and the way in which trainees were taught how to use it. Educationally, however, the *Clarence* boys were found to be below par. The total cost of running the ship for the year was £4,407 17s 8d.

Finances were always a problem for all three ships. Voluntary subscriptions or contributions from well-meaning benefactors invariably dropped off once the initial enthusiasm for the project had passed. In 1860, for example, while support for the new reformatories was still high, there were voluntary contributions – for all reformatories, not just the ships – of £24,903. By 1890 this figure had dropped to £2,793. Treasury contributions towards the upkeep and running of the schools rose from £59,230 in 1860 to £78,863 – an increase, but hardly a great one.[37]

The story of the reformatory school ships is a complex one and does not always make salutary reading. Over the years there were mutinies and assaults, arson attacks and outbreaks of typhoid and enteric fever. Scandal often seemed to hover over the ships like a giant black cloud – it is a topic we shall return to later.

CHAPTER FOUR
Industrial School Ships

The story of Britain's industrial schools is closely linked to that of the reformatories. They were established alongside each other following the 1854 Youthful Offenders Act and much of the energy that marked the early years of the reformatory movement was mirrored in the creation of the industrial schools.

A series of Industrial School Acts between 1856 and 1861 attempted to deal with the problem of destitute, homeless and disorderly children. These were Mary Carpenter's 'perishing' rather than 'dangerous' classes, youngsters who were not necessarily delinquent but who had problems with care and control. Without help they would, almost certainly, slip into a life of crime.

Beggars had been a problem since the Middle Ages. Not for nothing did the old rhyme 'Hark, hark, dogs do bark/Beggars are coming to town' cast a chill over the hearts and minds of people of substance. The Poor Law Acts of 1601 had attempted to solve the problem of vagrancy by placing responsibility for looking after the local poor on individual parishes. A Poor Rate had been levied and small workhouses established but, wherever possible, the poor were to be maintained in their own homes.

The end of the Napoleonic Wars in 1815 saw a huge rise in the number of unemployed suddenly thrown onto the Poor Relief. Bands of discharged soldiers and sailors, as well as dozens of redundant workers from the manufacturing industries, roamed the countryside, often terrorising honest citizens by their lawless behaviour. Almost in desperation, the Poor Law Amendment Act was passed, abolishing the practice of helping people in their own homes and concentrating them, instead, into large workhouses. The regimes in such places were prison-like with families being split and such work as was available being hard and degrading. The harshness was deliberate, deterrence from entering the workhouse always being the prime aim.

Following the mid-century reforms to the services available for delinquent youngsters, it was inevitable that there should also be some changes to those provided for their less intractable comrades. The new industrial schools were not designed for the incorrigible delinquents of the reformatories. The 1861 Act stated that the type of child best suited to these new schools was 'any child apparently under the age of fourteen years found begging or receiving alms, or being in any street or public place for the purpose of begging or receiving alms.'[38]

Juveniles found 'wandering' could also be admitted to the schools, if magistrates saw fit. So too could children who were disorderly or out of their parents' control. Children could be sent if their mothers had been convicted of a crime, if they were living with common or reputed prostitutes or it could be proved that they were being neglected in any way. In 1860, industrial schools were included under the remit of the Home Secretary and, thereafter, were virtually always spoken about in the same breath as the reformatories.

The origins, or at least the theoretical base, of industrial schools can be found in the 'ragged schools', which had been founded by John Pounds, a disabled cobbler from Portsmouth, early in the nineteenth century. At the age of fifty-two Pounds gathered together the poor children he encountered on the streets of Portsmouth and taught them the rudiments of reading and writing. Children were also instructed in a form of trade training – simple cookery for the girls, shoe making for the boys. Pounds' ragged school movement spread rapidly in the middle decades of the nineteenth century and by the time of the first Industrial School Acts most large cities or towns had felt the influence of at least one of his schools.

As with the reformatories, dozens of industrial schools sprang into existence once the legislation to create them had been enshrined in law. A committee of philanthropic or interested people – usually men – would be formed, with a view to providing a voluntary and self-funding school for a specific geographical area. The committees were usually made up of wealthy businessmen and people with significant church or chapel connections. They were all invariably individuals who had a vested interest in maintaining the structure of society and keeping everyone in their rightful place – the rich man in his castle, the poor man at his gate.

The primary aim of the schools, in keeping with the traditions of John Pounds' ragged schools, was to provide trade training. However, the need to self-fund often superseded any real value the system might have offered. Youngsters were more often employed in producing goods for sale (boots, shoes, clothes, vegetables) than they were in learning about the processes involved. It was, in many cases, little more than slave labour. Some parents objected strongly. Canon Girdlestone, giving evidence to the Newcastle Commission, was quick to point out that 'with regard to industrial work there is a good deal of dislike among the lower classes to their children being employed in such work, in the place of book learning'.[39] Despite his disparaging tone and condescending reference to 'the lower classes', there is no doubt he had a point. Many parents saw great value in education and wanted their children taught to read and write so that they could better themselves. Many others, though, either did not worry what happened in the schools or were simply relieved to have their unwanted offspring cared for by others.

Reformers and educationalists quickly came to the conclusion that, judging by the success of the reformatory school ships, sea-borne industrial training could also be a way forward. The Commission on Manning the Navy (1858) had

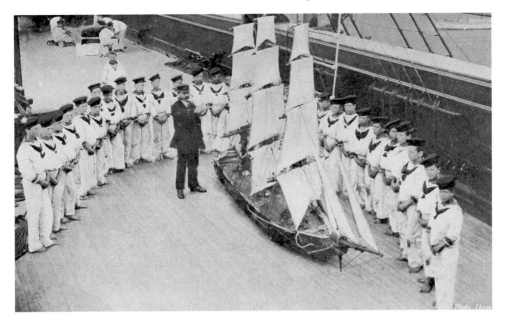

Instruction by model on the deck of a training ship.

The *Indefatigable* off Rock Ferry on the Mersey. Never a certificated industrial school, she still trained homeless and destitute boys.

already made the recommendation that, following serious problems in providing enough sailors during the Crimean War, school ships should be established in all major commercial ports. The commission had recommended 120 to 200 such ships, 100 of them to be State run. Such a proposal was idealistic and never really viable but while the commission did not intend to train delinquent or semi-delinquent boys –'the least likely to be amenable to discipline and most likely to abandon their country when most needed', according to Admiral Martin, one of the Commissioners – there were many philanthropists who did not agree.[40]

These reformers felt that a system, a fleet almost, of industrial school ships would do far more than keep unwanted children out of society's way. It would provide boys with skills that they could use when they finally left school. It was a feeling that was quickly approved of and backed by the government, a treasury grant of six shillings per head, per week being awarded to any organisation that decided to found and run an industrial school ship. The grant was never large but it did provide a regular and steady stream of income.

Nine industrial school ships – in the true sense of the term – were established. These were vessels created and run by voluntary bodies, aided by the treasury grant, catering for youngsters who had been sent by the courts, usually for periods of up to five years. These ships, their location and the date of their establishment are shown below:

Vessel	Location	Date Established
Havannah	Cardiff	1861
Wellesley	North Shields	1868
Southampton	Hull	1868
Cumberland/Empress	Helensburgh	1869
Mars	Dundee	1869
Formidable	Portishead	1869
Gibraltar	Belfast	1872
Clio	Bangor	1877
Mount Edgcumbe	Saltash	1877

The *Empress* replaced the *Cumberland* after an arson attack in 1889, being positioned at the same mooring on the Gareloch and offering the same service, albeit under a different name.

There were three other vessels that can be loosely grouped with the industrial ships, even though they were not run directly as schools of industry on a voluntary or subscription basis but as semi-official units of local government organisations. These were:

Indefatigable	Rock Ferry	1864
Goliath/Exmouth	Grays	1870
Shaftesbury	Grays	1878

A rare and faded view of the *Goliath*, destroyed by fire in December 1875. (courtesy of Thurrock History Museum, Grays).

Of these last three the *Indefatigable* was a training ship for homeless and destitute children – 'the honest poor', as Victorians would have said. Run by the Manchester and Salford Refuges, many Liverpool ship owners like John Clint and James Bibby had a hand in both its founding and running. The *Indefatigable* was never a certified school ship and therefore did not receive any form of government grant; the committee felt that such an award would lower the character of the vessel and hinder their running of the school. Moored off Rock Ferry on the Mersey, she lay for forty years within hailing distance of two other renowned training ships, the *Akbar* and the *Conway*.

One interesting feature of the *Indefatigable* was the floating swimming pool that was moored alongside the ship. Measuring 50 ft by 20 ft, it was an iron cellular structure, complete with adjustable bottom. A metal cruiser, the *Phaeton*, replaced the wooden *Indefatigable* during the First World War, although the name *Indefatigable* was retained. Transferred to the Menai Straits in 1940 in an effort to avoid the German bombing of Liverpool, the school duly moved ashore and ran until the end of the twentieth century, albeit as a public school with few, if any, nautical connections.

The *Goliath* was originally founded by the Hackney, Poplar and Whitechapel Poor Law Unions and attached to the Forest Gate District of the London School Board. Like the *Indefatigable* she did not receive a government grant and was not, therefore, an industrial ship in the truest sense of the term. Burned out at her moorings on 22 December 1875, she was replaced by the *Exmouth*, a new establishment that was run by the Metropolitan Asylums Board. Fitted out as a TS in the wake of the *Goliath* fire, she arrived off Grays in December 1876, just

The first *Exmouth*, replacement for the *Goliath*, shown here off Grays in the early years of the twentieth century.

twelve months after the end of her predecessor. She, in turn, was succeeded by a new *Exmouth* in 1905. From 1930 until the Second World War, the ship was run by the London County Council.

Life on the *Exmouth* was strict. It had to be with over 400 boys on board at any one time. However, conditions were not unduly cruel and should be taken in the context of the time. Boys were beaten when it was felt necessary but miscreants were usually punished by being given extra chores such as scrubbing the deck. As scrubbing was done on hands and knees, behind an officer hosing water and sprinkling sand, it was an unwelcome task that was a far more effective deterrent than a few strokes of the cane.

A letter from boy no. 6290, W. Lawrence, dated 1897, shows how humane the regime actually was. Capt Bourchier was approached by Lawrence, who had been discharged from the ship, asking that he might be readmitted. He wanted, he stated, 'another start in life as mother wishes me to go to the Merchant service . . . I wish I had not left the old *Exmouth*. I wish I was there now. I liked it very much and the officers was (*sic.*) very kind indeed'.[41] Lawrence was taken back on board and duly went to sea a few years later.

Built to resemble a wooden wall, the second *Exmouth* was actually a purpose-built, steel vessel with the advantage of having more headroom than any wooden warship. During the Second World War she was taken over by London's fire brigades, serving as a depot ship for several years. She was then towed to Scapa Flow where she spent time as a supply ship. Never having been intended for sea duties, she apparently rolled horrendously during the tow and was lucky not to sink. After the war *Exmouth* returned to the Thames where she replaced the officers training ship, *Worcester* – but more of this later.

The second *Exmouth* came to Grays in 1905 and is shown here in mid-stream shortly after her arrival. She was a purpose-built steel ship, designed to look like an old woodenwall.

The *Shaftesbury* was owned and run by the London School Board. Moored off Grays, she was formerly the P & O vessel, *Nubia*, operating on the London-to-Bombay run. She was an elegant ship, one that certainly provided more comfort for her inmates than most similar establishments, and was relatively successful as many of her trainees joined one of the major shipping companies or London's steam tug fleet on their discharge.

Bought for £7,000 after the Admiralty refused to loan the school board a ship, many of the boys for whom the *Shaftesbury* catered were habitual truants from the newly created board schools. The original certification registered her to take 500 boys but this was almost immediately reduced to 400 – more manageable, perhaps, but still a huge number of bodies in the confined space of an old wooden ship.

The *Shaftesbury* had the services of a topsail schooner, named the *Themis*. In the summer, this vessel would cruise up and down the Thames Estuary and often as far down the Channel as Plymouth. With a permanent crew of three, she could take up to thirty boys for valuable experience of life at sea.

The regimes and structures of the nine true industrial school ships were broadly similar to those of the reformatory ships. Home Office regulations were quite specific about the daily routines of such establishments – the threat of removing the treasury grant was always a sword to be held above the head of each committee – and, within certain limitations, most ships followed a fairly common programme.

Instruction was provided in reading, writing, spelling and number work for three hours each day. If there was time, some basic aspects of history, geography and drawing were also crammed in. Music was often given special attention and many of the ships possessed good brass bands. Much of the music the boys played was religious – as William Booth of the Salvation Army had said, 'Why should the Devil have all the best tunes?' – and there was always a need for musicians such as buglers and drummers, both in the Navy and the Army.

Industrial training concentrated on the basic aspects of navigation, on essential tasks such as mast climbing, on splicing and rope coiling, and on small boat work. Such training was usually given in the afternoons. Boys would rise at 6 a.m., possibly half an hour later in the winter, and begin the day with an act of worship. Lunch was usually taken at about 1.30, tea at 4.30 and lights out was at 8.30. If they were lucky, boys would be given an hour for recreation during the evening.

After 1875 each boy who was accepted into the Royal Navy earned his ship a bounty of £25. However, as well as having to meet a rigorous set of physical standards, in order to be accepted boys needed to have a good working knowledge of the sea and small boats. As a result of this requirement many industrial ships bought tenders, small sailing craft that could be used on short sea and estuary cruises.

Managers of the *Southampton* at Hull purchased the tender, *Ripple*, in 1878, and on this tiny vessel officers and boys undertook twenty-four-hour trips along the Humber and even out into the North Sea. The *Formidable* at Portishead had the *Polly*, and boys would regularly sail her as far down the Bristol Channel as Lundy Island. The *Mars* at Dundee was provided with the *Francis Mollison*. Under the command of Capt Scott, she was a common sight along the Scottish coast. Even the London County Council's *Exmouth* had a small tender, the 100-ton brig, *Steadfast*. This beautiful little vessel was replaced by another tender, the *Exmouth II*, in 1913.

As with the reformatory ships, all industrial school ships were inspected by the Home Office. There was a suggestion in the Aberdare Report that they should come under the auspices of the Education Department, but this would have meant that education would have to concern itself with issues such as remission of sentences. As a consequence the ships (and the schools) remained the responsibility of the Home Office. Annual reports were, therefore, more often concerned with care and control than education, even in the broadest sense. They were not very detailed; differences between good and bad schools were rarely identified and there was little attempt at critical appraisal.

Food on the ships was basic but filling. On the *Southampton* lunch was usually a hot meal of salt pork or fresh beef, preserved meat and soup. Vegetables, bread and biscuits were extras. Breakfast consisted of bread, biscuits and cocoa with oatmeal porridge being substituted every other day. Most of the ships followed a similar dietary pattern.

The *Havannah* at Cardiff was the first industrial school ship to be established. She was an historic vessel, having twice sailed around the world and been one of the vessels that escorted Napoleon Bonaparte into exile on St Helena in 1815. A grounded hulk, she was brought to Cardiff in 1860 when, for a while, she became

The *Shaftesbury*, originally the elegant ex P & O vessel *Nubia*, and run as an industrial
school ship by the London School Board.

the base for Cardiff's ragged school. The ragged school had opened five years
earlier, based on the site of the old cavalry barracks in Union Street. The decks of
the *Havannah* were considered far more appropriate premises.

One of the great supporters and advocates of an industrial school in the area
was Mary Carpenter. Still railing about the system that forced children to spend a
short period in prison before admission to a reformatory or industrial school, in
1860 she wrote in the *Cardiff and Merthyr Guardian* that it was 'a serious evil to
subject a child to the hardening effect of a public trial, and then to familiarity with
the secrets of the interior of those walls which should only be beheld with dread
from without . . . If such a school is needed in any part of the world it certainly
is at Cardiff'.[42]

Cardiff was then one of the premier ports in Britain, millions of tons of coal
being mined in the Rhondda Valley and exported through Cardiff Docks each
year. Poverty and delinquency, vagrancy and abuse, were rife in many parts of the
town. Sensing a real need, the Ragged School Committee made a request to the
Admiralty, asking for a suitable hulk on which to open an industrial school. After
much debate, the *Havannah* was donated, on the condition that the committee
shoulder the cost of towing her from the south coast to Cardiff and of fitting her
out as a school ship.

There was considerable argument about accepting the old wooden wall, which
had neither masts nor rigging but, eventually, it was decided to take her without
her yards and to 'house her over' instead. The *Havannah* was towed to Cardiff
by the steam tug *Iron Duke* and moored first in East Bute Docks. A large and
enthusiastic crowd greeted her arrival on 9 July 1860 – she was, at that stage, the
largest vessel to enter Cardiff Docks.

The members of the *Wellesley* Ship Band pose with their instruments – music was an important part of the curriculum on industrial ships.

It proved impossible for the organising committee to obtain permission for the *Havannah* to remain in East Bute Dock and as a result, on 17 September, she was towed to a muddy bank of the River Taff, on the south side of Penarth Road. A wooden bridge was built to connect her with the road and a huge, timber structure erected over her main deck. The result was an enormous Noah's Ark affair that sat, uneasy and ungainly, on the mud of the river for the next forty years. The first classes took place on 1 November 1860 while the ship was still registered as a ragged school. Only on 5 January 1862 did a certificate arrive, registering the *Havannah* as an industrial school ship.

The first compulsory admissions, true industrial school boys who had been sent by the courts, were received on board early that year. However, voluntary admissions – ragged school boys and girls – continued to attend for several months until the sheer pressure of referrals forced them to be discharged.

Although the ship was at least nominally aground, at high tides she would often float off the mud. Limestone ballast was shipped and, eventually, in 1866, huge embankments were built around the hulk. The boys dug vegetable patches in the enclosed area but the river still regularly washed in over the embankments, destroying much of their hard work. When the *Havannah* was first established she was alone, isolated on her mud bank. Over the years, however, houses and warehouses were built around her so that, gradually, the ship seemed to be engulfed by buildings.

Sydney Turner, who had moved from the Royal Philanthropic Reformatory at Redhill to the Home Office, inspected the ship in September 1866. He stated that 'the arrangements of the ship . . . seem to be just what one would wish – well calculated to exercise a good influence over the boys and to promote the great object of the institution, namely the weaning of the lads from those habits of vagrancy and disorder which are the beginnings of crime'.[43]

The original industrial school ship *Havannah*, shown here on an early print before she was taken to Cardiff in her new role.

Twenty years later, however, the 30th Report of the Inspector of Reformatory and Industrial Schools did not paint such a rosy picture. Then the inspector commented that 'the institution, discipline and training are grossly inefficient . . . the boys are greatly addicted to both lying and thieving; and their health is much tried in consequence of the insalubrity (*sic.*) of the swampy location'.[44]

The ship's original bosun was William Jayne. An irascible man who ruled with an iron rod, he held the schoolmaster superintendents – the *Havannah* Committee had always been unable to find a naval man to run the ship – in utter contempt. There was continuous friction that resulted in Jayne resigning in April 1870. What little nautical training there had been went with him. The 13th Report of the *Havannah* Committee (1867) showed that out of six leavers that year, one had gone to sea. The report for 1870, after Jayne's departure, put the figure at one out of eleven leavers. In 1882 that figure went up to eight but between 1887 and 1889 not one boy took up the sea option when his time for discharge arrived.[45]

The second industrial school ship, the *Wellesley*, was certificated at North Shields on the River Tyne on 25 July 1868. By 1873, there were 240 boys on board, the ship having been approved for 300. The vessel herself was actually the first *Cornwall*, the old reformatory ship that had served on the Thames and which had been literally 'swopped' by the *Cornwall* Committee when they felt she had become too small and cramped for their purposes. A sum of £4,000 was now spent on alterations, £2,000 having been raised at a bazaar in Newcastle town hall. This first *Wellesley* survived until 1875 when she was replaced by a larger ship.

One of the earliest captain superintendents of the *Wellesley* was Comd. Charles Ashwell Botcher Pocock. He lived on the ship with his family, his daughter, Lena, being actually born on board in 1872. Like many who were engaged in reformation work, Pocock was profoundly religious and ruled the boys with a rod of iron until he resigned his post in 1880.

One of the complaints about industrial ships was the fact that they often took boys of any age, regardless of their physical condition. In an attempt to rectify this situation Green's Home was opened in 1885 as part of the *Wellesley* establishment. The Home catered for up to sixty boys who would be accommodated and helped there until they reached the age of twelve when, if appropriate, they could be transferred to the ship to begin their nautical training.

When the *Southampton* arrived at Hull in 1868 she had come without masts, spars, rigging or boats. These were valuable assets and had, as with most other ships loaned or given by the Admiralty, been removed for use on other Royal Navy ships. The Committee of the Humber Training Ship Southampton for Homeless and Destitute Boys had to purchase these items, a transaction that cost them over £3,000. An appeal was made and donations came flooding in. By the time of the first AGM of the committee the debt had been reduced to £1,100.[46]

Registered for 200 boys, by January 1870 the *Southampton* had 127 youngsters on board. The first captain superintendent was Capt Pollard RN and from the beginning there were serious disturbances. An arson attempt was thwarted in

January 1874 when a bowl of tar and a quantity of wood were discovered below the water-line. In retaliation at the discovery, boys threw forty-two pairs of trousers, bedding, rugs and other clothing overboard. The police were called, six constables going onto the ship to restore order. On 26 January, Henry Pidgeon, Thomas Maddon, Timothy Harrington and Robert Brown were all charged with attempting to sink the *Southampton* and packed off to a reformatory school.

Things improved gradually. Capt Pollard refused to take an overly punitive stance and, once one or two of the less effective instructors moved on, the ship settled down to a regular routine. Hull was certainly proud of its training ship and regular sight-seeing trips around the *Southampton*, at a charge of one shilling and sixpence per head, were soon organised. Severe damage was caused to the ship in the winter of 1870/71 when ice banging into the hull caused several seams to spring. As a result, after 1885 the *Southampton* always wintered in Alexandra Dock. This was a unique arrangement as normally the training ships were moored in one spot and remained there for the rest of their useful lives.

Scotland was well represented by training ships. To begin with there was the *Cumberland*, established in 1869 at Helensburgh on the Gareloch. The brainchild of a dozen or so Scottish businessmen, she was originally intended to take 400 boys but the number was reduced to 360 and by the end of her first year there were 150 on board.

The *Cumberland* was a relatively new ship, having been launched in 1842 and becoming an early victim of the Royal Navy's move towards iron rather than wooden ships. Her life as a training vessel was equally as short as on 18 February 1889, with 390 boys and crew on board, she was destroyed by an arson attack. She was replaced by the *Empress* – formerly HMS *Revenge* – and boys, who had been temporarily housed ashore, simply transferred to the new ship.

Another Scottish industrial ship was the *Mars*. Moored on the Tay at Dundee, she was certificated on 30 September 1869, being intended to train 400 boys from the west coast of Scotland. The inspector's report for 1889 records that there was a full complement of boys on board and that 185 of them were Catholic. The same report commented that an iron roof had been built over the fore part of the upper deck. Telephone connections to both sides of the River Tay were a useful safety feature while the lower decks could, if necessary, be flooded in minutes from tanks on the upper ones.[47] Obviously the recent destruction of the *Cumberland* was weighing heavily on the mind of that particular inspector.

An important part of the *Mars* establishment, lying a short distance away along the riverbank, were a large playing field, a garden and a hospital/sick-bay. There was a tender, *Lightning*, – soon to be replaced by the *Francis Mollison* – and, interestingly, an auxiliary home at 219 Penarth Road in far-off Cardiff. This was not, perhaps, as strange as it might seem. Cardiff was an exceptionally busy port and virtually all merchant sailors could expect to call there, perhaps three or four times a year. Maintaining a home or hostel for old *Mars* boys was a caring gesture and provided somewhere they could be sure of a warm bed and clean sheets and blankets.

Built over to resemble a gigantic Noah's Ark, the *Havannah* was the only Industrial Ship not to be afloat – although when the high tides of the Bristol Channel rushed in she often floated clear of her mud bank.

The 1871 report of the *Mars* Committee stated, 'Of the boys now on board 69 are orphans; 109 are fatherless; 51 have been deserted by their parents. They all come from the poorest class, and it is probable that the largest number of them would have fallen into crime.'[48]

Boys attended classes for formal education on alternate days, the rest of their time being taken up with nautical training. They carried out gun and rifle drill, worked at splicing and manoeuvring small boats along the river. In addition, they made and mended their own clothes and trained in alternative occupations such as carpentry and shoe making. This alternative style of education was a suggestion of J. G. Legge, Chief Inspector of Reformatory and Industrial Schools, and was an acknowledgement that not all the boys on board the *Mars* would take to the sea as a career.

The *Formidable* was moored 400 yards off Portishead Pier near Bristol, receiving her certificate in November 1869. Earlier that year a provisional committee had been convened to look at the possibility of providing a training ship for homeless and destitute boys from the Bristol area. One of the committee, Mr H. Fedden, was delegated to visit the reformatory ships on the Thames and Mersey, to see what he could discover. He reported back that he had been impressed by the quality of work he witnessed and the idea of a similar type of ship for Bristol should be supported.

From June 1868 the *Wellesley* lay at North Shields on the Tyne – until she was destroyed by fire in 1914.

The *Formidable*, then lying at Sheerness, was donated by the Admiralty and was towed to Portishead in September 1869. Her first captain superintendent was to be Capt E. Poulden RN. Charles Kingsley, author of *The Water Babies*, performed the opening ceremony on 2 October and the first ten boys arrived on board during November. During her first ten years as training ship, the *Formidable* received 1,046 boys, 502 of them going on to join either the Royal or Merchant Navies.

The ship was always well run and clean. During the full length of her career she reported only eighteen deaths on board, a lower number than any other training ship in the country. Death was a common occurrence on the ships, either from accident or from disease. In 1889, for example, *Clarence* reported two deaths, *Cornwall* three and even the enlightened regime of the *Mars* was forced to acknowledge that no fewer than eight boys had succumbed between 1886 and 1888.

Boys on the *Formidable* were organised into two watches, one receiving nautical training while the other went to school. Then the watches simply changed around. Discipline was harsh and included corporal punishment by the use of birch rod and solitary confinement on restricted rations.

Ireland's training ship was the *Gibraltar*, moored at Belfast. She received her certificate in June 1872 and was registered to take 350 boys. She was not a great success, however, and closed after just twenty-seven years, in 1899. There had already been something of a problem and in the late 1880s the school seems to have briefly suspended its service. The ship was renamed *Grampian* and was loaned again to the Belfast Training Ship Committee in 1889 before being finally towed away for breaking ten years later.

The closure was not without some censure, William Johnson commenting on the matter in Parliament: 'I beg to ask the First Lord of the Admiralty if he is

With Best Wishes
    for Christmas.

Hull's training ship was the *Southampton*, arriving off the port in 1868 without masts, spars or rigging. The Committee's first job was to raise money to provide these.

An artist's impression of the *Cumberland*, moored at Helensburgh on the Clyde.

The *Cumberland* was burned to the waterline in 1889 and was duly replaced by the *Empress*.

The *Mars* lay on the River Tay. Like the *Havannah* at Cardiff, part of her upper deck was housed over to provide classrooms for the boys.

The *Formidable*, off Portishead, was one of the most successful of the industrial ships, regularly placing most of her leavers into positions at sea.

The Belfast industrial ship *Gibraltar*, an early print from *The Illustrated London News*, 8 February 1873.

Boys rowing out to the Bangor training ship *Clio*. The *Clio*, a *Racoon*-class corvette, had circumnavigated the world twice before she arrived in the Menai Straits in her new role.

The *Mount Edgcumbe*, Training Ship of the Devonport and Cornwall Industrial Ship Association.

Music, music, music – boys of the *Mount Edgcumbe* Band.

aware of the great dissatisfaction and disappointment caused in Belfast and the neighbourhood by the disinclination on the part of the Government to place a training ship in Belfast Lough.'[49]

Whether or not there was any real dissatisfaction in Belfast is a matter of conjecture. The government response was off-hand and low-key. Ships like the *Gibraltar* were run by voluntary bodies and if they were not being used then that was a matter for the individual committee, not the State! Certainly the ship had been low on numbers for years and nobody seemed inclined to send boys for training. The rural nature of Ireland, where problem children were invariably dealt with by the small, tightly knit communities in which they lived, undoubtedly played a part in the failure of the ship. Then, of course, the shipyards of Belfast offered hard, grinding but financially rewarding employment for the young men of the city.

Wales enjoyed the services of another industrial ship, apart from the *Havannah*. This was the *Clio*, moored off Bangor Pier in August 1877 after almost eighteen months of fund-raising. The original idea was to place a training ship in the River Dee but it was feared that locating a ship there would only hold back boys from worthwhile labour in the collieries of the area. So the Menai Straits was chosen as an alternative.

The *Clio* was a small ship, a *Racoon*-class corvette that had twice circumnavigated the globe. Her official opening took place on 20 August when the band of the *Indefatigable* played for the guests. There was great excitement about the ship and the job it had to do, essays being written at that year's National Eisteddfod in Caernarfon about the value of nautical training. In December there were just

Music was one of the few subjects taught on board all industrial school ships. The theory was that the army and navy would always need musicians.

seven boys on board, but by the end of January 1878 there were fifty-four on roll.

The West Country also had its own training ship. This was the *Mount Edgcumbe*, which received her Home Office certificate on 29 August 1877 and was moored virtually beneath the famous railway bridge at Saltash. The ship had previously served as the officer training ship, *Conway*, on the Mersey, being handed over to the newly formed Devonport and Cornwall Industrial Training Ship Association in July 1876. The Earl of Mount Edgcumbe, off whose land the vessel was moored, was president of the committee.

The *Mount Edgcumbe* was never very successful in placing boys into positions at sea and it is hard to account for this failing. Situated close to Devonport and Plymouth, this was a sailor's region and the expectation was that needy boys would be eager to avail themselves of the service. The influence of the Royal Navy was strong and there was a real passion for the Navy amongst most local lads. Possibly the very popularity of the Navy worked against the *Mount Edgcumbe*. Most boys had set their sights on the Royal Navy – the Merchant Navy was very much a secondary option. With such a huge catchment group, the Royal Navy could afford to be choosy. The *Mount Edgcumbe* boys did not really stand much of a chance.

The inspector's report for 1889 recorded that there were 178 boys on board, the inspector commenting on the hospital and playing field close by on shore. One boy had died after falling into the hold and three boys had been discharged because of poor health – a most unusual occurrence on a training ship. Educationally, the school had improved since the previous inspection, although writing was, in many cases, defective. The comment was made that 'a good deal of the indifferent writing must be attributed to defective desk accommodation, many of the boys having to hold their slates on their knees.'[50]

Taken as a whole, the work of the industrial school ships was never totally effective. A Notice of Motion by Adml Field in March 1895 was nothing short of condemnatory. He regarded the ships as being extravagant and wasteful. According to Field, many of the boys would never go to sea and should never have been sent to a training ship in the first place. He was particularly vitriolic about the *Havannah*, believing that its boys were half fed and that it was 'the worst specimen of these naval industrial ships . . . the hulk ought to be burnt and everybody connected with it discharged immediately'.[51] The Home Office agreed with some of Adml Field's comments and set up a system of transfers where unsuitable boys could be moved off the ships to land-based schools. They also agreed to limit the age of boy trainees to twelve years.

The research of Inspector Henry Rogers into the disposal of industrial ship boys between 1888 and 1890 shows that Adml Field was not far wrong in many of his assertions. The ships were clearly not meeting their aim of giving boys careers at sea. What the research does not do is take account of those who might have been saved from a life of crime by being placed on one of the ships, nor does it take into account the numbers of boys who went into allied professions, such as the Army.

Ships	1888 Discharges	1888 To sea	1889 Discharges	1889 To sea	1890 Discharges	1890 To sea	Percentage
Clio	57	31	64	36	66	42	58.28%
Mount Edgcumbe	83	18	62	18	62	21	27.53%
Wellesley	85	58	74	57	81	54	70.41%
Shaftesbury	125	48	100	41	137	71	44.19%
Formidable	83	64	107	77	109	86	75.92%
Southampton	72	49	61	34	66	29	56.28%
Empress	119	85	130	93	125	78	68.45%
Mars	135	69	132	49	133	71	47.25%

Interestingly, Rogers did not include either the *Havannah* or the *Gibraltar* in his figures. Their returns would have undoubtedly made the statistics even worse.

Taking the above figures into consideration it would seem that the overall percentage of industrial ship boys who went to sea between 1888 and 1890 – which must be viewed as a fairly typical period – was 56.04 per cent, only just over half of the total number of discharges. When the poor *Mount Edgcumbe* figures are taken out of the calculation the total still rises to only 60.11 per cent. As training on the ships cost approximately 20 per cent more than that in land-based schools many people came to consider it a bad investment.[52]

The 1913 report of the Departmental Committee on Reformatory and Industrial Schools tried to break down the actual destinations of boys leaving the training ships by looking at disposals in one particular period. At the end of 1911 only 163 ship boys had, that year, gone into the Royal Navy; 246 had joined the Merchant Navy; 51 were involved in coastal trade (i.e. barges, tugs, etc.); 52 were employed on fishing boats. By contrast, 538 had joined the army.[53]

These facts and figures were all the more worrying when other schools were examined. Several years before, Sydney Turner had praised the work of the Middlesex Industrial School at Feltham. This school had a nautical section of 120 boys. Carefully selected and trained, using the land-locked replica ship, *Endeavour*, no more than 10 per cent of this select group failed to enter either the Royal or Merchant Navies.

Even those boys who did go to sea faced a great personal crisis before, during and after their first voyage. They undertook menial work on board their ships, were usually seasick and treated with contempt or abused by the other sailors. When they returned from a voyage they had money in their pockets for the first time in their lives. This they would quickly spend and, needing cash while waiting for another berth, would drift into other jobs, effectively turning their backs on the sea. However, if they did manage to make a second cruise then there was a fair likelihood that they would go on to make a career out of seafaring. All too often this did not happen, Home Office figures showing that out of 448 boys sent to sea in 1910, only 170 were still working afloat in 1913.[54]

It is difficult to work out why one ship should have been more successful than another, why the *Formidable*, for example, should be able to consistently send half to three-quarters of its boys to sea while the *Mount Edgcumbe* and *Havannah* failed to provide more than a handful each year. If the training ship happened to be situated close to a fishing port then that was often the best and most productive outlet for the boys. The *Southampton* is a good example, being based close to several important fishing ports. By 1884 there were twenty skippers, forty second hands and seventy third hands sailing out of Hull and Grimsby who had once been inmates on board the Hull school ship.[55] At the end of the day it invariably came down to the quality of staff available and often, when a good captain superintendent or bosun left his post, the success rate of a particular ship dropped accordingly.

Industrial school ships were an attempt to provide boys at risk with an acceptable and rewarding way out of the poverty trap. They tried to offer more than just a punitive regime, trying to guide each boy towards a useful career where he would not become a drain on society. They were never wholly successful but even a 50 per cent success rate was better than nothing and the alternative was too costly and too troubling for Victorian Britain to ever seriously consider.

CHAPTER FIVE
Charity and Voluntary Training Ships

Building on the initial success – or apparent success – of the reformatory and industrial ships, the second half of the nineteenth century saw the establishment of what can be loosely called charity or voluntary training ships. These were vessels provided by voluntary agencies or, in some cases, by private individuals, ships that were not intended for delinquent or even semi-delinquent boys. Rather, they catered for those youngsters who had little or no inclination towards crime or vagrancy but who needed help in order to survive in the harsh world of Victorian and Edwardian Britain. The clientele of these ships were, by and large, boys who wished to better themselves. In some cases they had parents who were actually prepared to pay for suitable training in order to make this happen.

With this type of trainee the charity ships were not certain of success but they certainly had a better chance than establishments where children were sent by the courts with no option other than to stay and see what fate had brought them. Most of the boys in these schools desperately wanted to be there. They knew that the sea would provide them with a future career.

The most famous of these ships were the *Chichester* and *Arethusa*, owned and run by the Shaftesbury Society. The society's origins date from the year 1843 when a disabled solicitor's clerk called William Williams, on a train journey to the west country, encountered a dozen or so boys, in rags, handcuffed and bound for transportation to Australia. Determined to do something about the effects of poverty that had brought the boys to this, Williams and a group of friends founded a ragged school in the notorious Seven Dials area of London. Before long Williams' project attracted the attention of the philanthropic Earl of Shaftesbury and this great social reformer soon became the prime mover in the ragged school movement. However, Shaftesbury wanted more.

On 14 February 1866, he extended an open invitation to the homeless boys of London asking them to come to a supper at St Giles Refuge. Over 150, all under the age of sixteen, responded to the invitation and turned up at St Giles 'at seven-o-clock, an hour before the proper time, they presented a miserable spectacle, with garments tattered and torn, and rather hanging about their limbs than covering them'.[56]

Most of the boys who attended the supper scavenged a living in the poorer districts of London. Nearly all of them were homeless, many having been abandoned by uncaring parents at an early age. It was a wonder they had not already fallen foul of the criminal justice system and many were inevitably operating on the fringes of delinquency. After supper had been eaten, Lord Shaftesbury stood up and posed the boys a question – would they be interested in living on board a ship and being trained for life in the Royal or Merchant Navies? The answer was an unqualified 'Yes!'

The Times newspaper gave both support and publicity to the scheme and a request for the loan or donation of a ship was made to the Admiralty. The fifty-gun *Chichester* was duly offered. She had never seen active service and was tiny, considering the huge number of boys who had expressed an interest, but she would do. On 6 November 1866, Shaftesbury noted in his diary, 'Today to Poplar to see ship in preparation for our school. It has been a dream of fifteen years and more. We have dashed on and are ready for action.'[57]

Inauguration of the *Chichester* took place on 20 December. The vessel was moored at Greenhithe and the work began. It had cost £5,000 to repair and fit out the ship, the money being donated by Baroness Burdett-Coutts, the noted philanthropist and friend of both Shaftesbury and Charles Dickens.

In 1874, a second, rather larger training ship joined *Chichester*. This was the famed *Arethusa*. By 1880, *Chichester* had been relegated to the role of drill ship with all the boys being accommodated on board the new vessel. The *Chichester* did not survive much longer, being sold off in May 1889 and broken up shortly afterwards.

Discipline on board the *Arethusa* was tough but fair and food, as on all the training ships, was nothing if not basic. Breakfast in these early years consisted of half a roll and a basin of cocoa, without either sugar or milk. Dinner was made up of small pieces of scorched mutton with boiled potatoes, cooked in their skins. Tea was another roll, accompanied by a large jug of milk-less and sugarless tea. In later years porridge, bread and margarine became the staple breakfast diet.

In 1880, the year that the original *Chichester* was superseded by the *Arethusa*, a small 120-ton tender was bought by the society. Christened *Chichester*, in honour of the original first ship, she was used solely for sea training, up to thirty boys at a time being taken down the Thames estuary and out into the North Sea. It was, perhaps, the best piece of training they received during their time on the *Arethusa*.

Boys in training wore serge trousers and flannel shirts, with serge outer jumpers if the weather became really harsh. Nobody was given boots until they had been at least six months on board when, it was felt, they would be less likely to run away. Within a few years of the ships being moored at Greenhithe, classrooms and playing fields were established on shore, close to the riverbank.

The *Arethusa* lay at Greenhithe until 1932. By this time, of course, she was old and in very poor condition. Consequently, the German-built *Peking* was bought for the sum of £6,500. A four-masted, steel-hulled barque, she was an impressive

Physical drill on the deck of the *Arethusa* – note, no boots on the boys.

The *Arethusa*, peaceful and still in the afternoon sunlight.

The second *Chichester*, dressed overall, a sketch from *The Quiver* magazine, 1876.

looking vessel and, being considerably larger than the *Arethusa*, promised well for the future comfort and training of the boys. By this stage the trainees were no longer the 'waifs and strays' that Shaftesbury and William Williams had first tried to help. As the Managing Committee was quick to point out, by the 1930s the ship catered only 'for boys of good character'.

For a brief period the *Peking* and *Arethusa* lay alongside each other in the Thames, the new vessel having arrived on station on 17 October 1932. However, by the end of 1934, the old *Arethusa* was in too bad a state for further use and she was sold off and broken up. There had, however, already been problems with her replacement. At 322 ft in length she was considerably larger than the old ship and this, combined with difficulties that arose over the site of the shore buildings that were now wanted for other purposes, meant that the mooring off Greenhithe was no longer viable.

As a result the *Peking*, now renamed *Arethusa*, was moved to Upnor on the Medway. The formal inauguration took place on Tuesday 25 July 1933. At the time of the move a staggering 12,302 boys had passed through the society's various ships, many of them going on to make good careers for themselves at sea. Even those who chose not to take the sea option seemed to have done well in their chosen careers, whether in the Army or civilian life.

Despite the undoubted success of the Shaftesbury Society and its ships there was always a considerable degree of bullying on board, both formal and informal. Jack Lacey, an ex-'Aree' boy, has recorded his comments: 'Mess robbing and an amount of bullying was tolerated as being, I suspect, good for character building. There was an obsession with scrubbing decks, ladders and the polishing of brass ... The fact that we seldom wore boots helped keep them immaculate. Indeed, in the year that I was aboard, mine were never repaired.'[58]

Discipline was never as repressive as it usually was on the reformatory and industrial ships but it was undoubtedly strict. Corporal punishment was used sparingly but it remained an option, twelve cuts across the buttocks being the maximum punishment allowed. Beaching – or being put ashore – was considered a far more fearful form of retribution.

The work of the Marine Society has already been mentioned. It was for many years something of a major rival to the ships of the Shaftesbury Society, the *Warspite* occupying a mooring off Charlton Pier. Launched in 1807 as a 3rd Rate, she had been loaned to the Marine Society in 1862, but on the morning of 3 January 1876 she was destroyed by fire as she lay at her moorings. Within a year the Admiralty had offered the *Conqueror* as a replacement. Her original name had been *Waterloo* and now, at the behest of the Marine Society, she was rechristened yet again, this time taking the traditional society name of *Warspite*. On 11 August 1901, she was moved down river to Greenhithe, keeping close company with the Shaftesbury Society's *Arethusa*.

Almost from the time of its first training ship, the Marine Society had employed schoolmasters on its vessels so that boys, as well as learning the art of seamanship and navigation, were also instructed in English, mathematics, scripture and music.

Apart from those who have entered the Royal Navy, over 7,000 of the boys who have passed through the Training Ship "Arethusa" have joined the Merchant Navy.

THE
SHAFTESBURY HOMES
and
"ARETHUSA" TRAINING SHIP

1,100 children are always being maintained.

FUNDS URGENTLY NEEDED.

Please remember the great work of the Training Ship "Arethusa," which has given so many poor boys a training to enable them to join the Royal Navy and Merchant Navy, and thus help to maintain the great traditions of those Services.

Patrons: THEIR MAJESTIES THE KING AND QUEEN; H.R.H. PRINCESS MARY, COUNTESS OF HAREWOOD; FIELD-MARSHAL H.R.H. THE DUKE OF CONNAUGHT. President: H.R.H. THE PRINCE OF WALES, K.G. Chairman and Treasurer: FRANCIS H. CLAYTON, ESQ. Deputy Chairman: LORD DARYNGTON. Chairman of "Arethusa" Committee: HOWSON F. DEVITT, ESQ. Secretary: F. BRIAN PELLY, A.F.C.

164 Shaftesbury Avenue, London, W.C.2

Right: An undated advertisement for the Shaftesbury Homes and the training ship *Arethusa* – according to the advert 1,100 children were being constantly maintained by the Society.

Below: The new *Arethusa*, previously the *Peking*, lying off Upnor. The figurehead of the old ship sits on the riverbank.

By 1940, in just less than 200 years of operations, the Marine Society had provided 39,910 men and 36,047 boys for service in the Royal Navy. In addition, it had sent no fewer than 34,776 boys into the Merchant Marine. Those are incredible figures that show not just the value of the society but also the lure of the sea in those busy and dangerous years.

The *Mercury* was another well-known charity school ship, having been founded in 1885 by Charles Hoare. The story behind the ship is one of scandal and disgrace and is irrevocably linked to the powerful, dynamic and brutal figure of Beatie Sumner. Born in 1862, Beatie met Charles Hoare on the hunting field and within weeks they were lovers. Coming from a wealthy family, Hoare was strong-willed, stubborn and, as a child, widely considered 'impossible'. He and Beatie Sumner were exactly alike.

Hoare was a good sportsman, excelling at cricket, tennis and horse riding. He was also a fine yachtsman and owned a number of small boats. These he kept moored at Exmouth where he often used them to offer training to local boys who then went on to find jobs on other yachts. A few of them even went into the Royal Navy.

The affair between Hoare and Beatie Sumner soon became public knowledge, creating a major society scandal as he was already married and had a number of children. Beatie's parents even made her a Ward of Court in an effort to keep the lovers apart. It was no use. An illegitimate daughter, Sybil, was born in 1884 and Hoare was taken to court. He could easily have been sent to prison and there was a huge amount of bad publicity for both him and his family. His wife refused him a divorce but left the family home, taking with her Hoare's sons and daughter.

In the summer of 1885 Hoare decided to found a training school. It was, in many respects, a philanthropic gesture, a way of making public amends. He had always been interested in nautical training and also probably decided that such a project would give Beatie some purpose in life.

That summer, in London Docks, Hoare found the barque, *Illova*. He bought her, renamed her *Mercury* and began to fit her out. The ship was small – she had been intended for work on the African coast and needed to be shallow draughted in order to cross sand bars at the river mouths. Now Hoare converted her into an exact replica of an early nineteenth-century warship. He also bought a topsail schooner, *Diana*, just 41 tons, to be used as a tender and as a cruiser for summer months.

A staff of fifteen was recruited and the first boys, 'street arabs' of about fourteen or fifteen years of age, were brought on board. At this stage Hoare bore most of the costs himself, eking out the funding with voluntary subscriptions from friends and acquaintances and, when needed, by specific fund-raising. The ship was moved from the Thames and moored off the village of Binstead on the Isle of Wight, Hoare and Beatie moving into a large house between the tideline and the village church.

Beatie was clear that discipline and control on board were to be maintained by example, and she was going to be the one to provide that example. Having

Boys of the Marine Society march behind their band along the deck of the *Warspite*.

A good shore establishment, working alongside the ship, was essential if the best value was to be obtained. This photograph shows the buildings of the Marine Society at Greenhithe.

been a wilful child and a determined adolescent herself, it was as if she had suddenly recognised the dangers of such strong personality traits in young people. She quickly mastered the sailors' skills and soon, wearing men's clothes so that movement about the ship would be easier, she was climbing rigging and rowing boats as well as any of the instructors. She sculled out to the *Mercury* every morning ay 6 a.m. and was invariably there for the rest of the day.

In October 1890 a reporter from *The Isle of Wight Observer* visited the ship. He found the vessel alive with activity: 'Small boys, newcomers to the ranks, were exercising with dumb-bells in one corner of the main deck . . . Lessons in seamanship took place on deck, and the whole ship was their classroom.'[59]

Every boy was given the opportunity to learn to play a brass or percussion instrument. Those who did not have the aptitude either sang or danced. One of the early music teachers was James McGavin, originally the ship's tailor, a man who played both the accordion and the tin whistle. So successful was his musical teaching that just three years after the ship opened for business a recreation hall was built above the shoreline, a place where lessons could be held and concerts given.

In October 1888, the *Mercury* surprisingly hoisted her anchor and sailed away to sea. Intended as an exercise to prove that the ship was no mere plaything for Hoare and Beatie, the cruise was a calculated gamble. Taking a ship full of trainees out to sea was a risky business, as Hoare and Beatie must have known. The *Eurydice*, a Royal Navy training brig carrying a crew of 350, had sunk off the Isle of Wight in 1878 – only two of the crew survived. Two years later the *Atalanta*, with a crew of over 200 – most of them boys in training – simply disappeared in the Atlantic. She left Bermuda and was never seen again. These were disasters that must have worried Charles Hoare but, despite his doubts, that autumn the *Mercury* sailed away.

The cruise was not quite a disaster but it was not far off. Boys had no idea where they were going and were constantly seasick as the *Mercury* headed down the Channel. The ship also leaked like a sieve and there was a serious problem with her rudder. However, they sailed on, through the Straits of Gibraltar and into the Mediterranean. It was Easter Sunday 1889 before the *Mercury* resumed her mooring off the Isle of Wight.

It was a short stay. In the Spring of 1892 the whole *Mercury* establishment moved to a site on the River Hamble in Hampshire. Here, on the riverbank, Charles Hoare bought playing fields and built classrooms and other permanent buildings. By 1896 a thriving community was in existence. A four-storey mansion was created for Hoare and Beatie and the Building – a huge theatre capable of holding 300 people – was fully operational. By now the old *Mercury* was moored in mid-stream and used solely as sleeping accommodation for the boys.

By the early years of the twentieth century the *Mercury* had abandoned her role as a charity school for needy boys. An advertisement from 1898 had already indicated that fees of £20 per annum were now payable and it was clear, for anyone who cared to see, that the establishment was inching closer and closer

Charles Hoare, the founder and first Captain-Superintendent of the *Mercury*.

The *Mercury* lies easily off shore.

The *Mercury* occupied a rural and isolated spot on the River Hamble, as this postcard view shows.

Mercury boys taking part in Morris Dancing, *c.* 1913.

Mercury boys march past, complete with field gun. Could the officer at the head of the column be the infamous Sharkey?

to becoming a minor public school. Following the death of Charles Hoare in 1907, the appointment of C. B. Fry, the England cricketer and world famous sportsman, to the position of captain superintendent clearly sealed the change of direction. Fry had married Beatie in June 1898, her long affair with Charles Hoare seeming to have withered away several years before.[60] With Fry as 'the front man' effective control of the *Mercury* now rested in Beatie Sumner's formidable hands. In the years to come she was to create a brutal and punishing regime that, at times, seemed to verge on the ludicrous and at others to come perilously close to sadism.

Within six months of Hoare's death, a governing body was appointed and *Mercury* was formally established as an educational charity. C. B. Fry's prime concerns were sport and journalism and these seemed to occupy him most of the time. Beatie, clearly aware of the Royal Navy bounty of £25 for every boy who entered the service, began to narrow the curriculum in order to ensure success. In good years the *Mercury* – and Beatie – received an income of over £1,000 from this source alone. Yet such success did not come without a price.

Whereas life on the *Mercury* had previously been similar to that in a large family, complete with room for individuality and personal choice, now discipline became the most important factor in the school. For Beatie it had become a guiding force that ruled her life, and the lives of all those around her: 'She had a loathing, containing a distinct element of fear, of boys being idle or even momentarily out of her control.'[61] Boys were watched constantly, even their toilet arrangements being carefully monitored. 'Too long at heads' became a major crime as Beatie automatically assumed they were engaged in activities other than

Left: Luxury was almost unheard of on the *Mercury*. But Market Day, when the boys could buy sweets with their pocket money, was eagerly awaited.

Below: The landlocked Training Ship *James Arthur*, Quarriers' Homes at Bridge of Weir.

Despite the idyllic, almost rural nature of this photograph, the *Stork* was actually moored off Hammersmith.

toileting! Corporal punishment was inflicted for a wide variety of offences, such beatings sometimes taking place across the breach of an old six-inch gun that had been cemented onto a platform in the corner of the gymnasium. Beatie decided who was to be flogged and up to twenty-four strokes were administered, each of them expertly placed on a different spot on the boy's backside by Arthur Ward, an ex-petty officer who was known throughout the school as 'Sharkey'.

The school had many strange rituals, all instituted by Beatie. During inspections boys had to bend down in unison and pull up their trouser legs so that she could inspect their bootlaces. On the order 'Show teeth' boys 'held out the left hand in a mad parody of the Nazi salute and brought the right hand up so that the toothbrush reposed, bristles outwards, against the bottom lip. At the same time they bared their front teeth in a hideous grin.'[62]

By 1908, the old *Mercury* was in a poor state of repair and Fry and Beatie applied to the Admiralty for a new vessel. It took several years, and then only after the personal intervention of the First Sea Lord, Winston Churchill, before the old RNR Drill Ship *President* was delivered to the Hamble.

The regime at *Mercury* was undoubtedly harsh and cruel, probably owing much to the repressed sexuality of Beatie Sumner – she and Fry had never had a particularly passionate relationship. But it did turn out excellent seamen, as Churchill himself admitted on a visit to the school in 1914. Whatever her faults – and there were many of them – Beatie certainly knew how to train sailors.

For a long while, Scotland had a charity school ship of a most unusual style. This was the *James Arthur*, which was stationed at Quarrier's Home in Bridge of Weir, many miles from the sea. Built on dry land and never intended to float,

Boys rigging sheer legs and derricks on the deck of the *Stork*.

she was not dissimilar from the *Fame* at Greenwich and the Middlesex industrial school's *Endeavour*.

William Quarrier was one of Scotland's leading philanthropists in the nineteenth century. He had begun his charity work in Glasgow where he founded a Shoe-Black Brigade that gave jobs and a purpose in life to many of the city poor. He built the City Orphanage but soon decided that needy children required fresh air and the open countryside. Consequently, he opened the Orphan Homes of Scotland at Bridge of Weir, deep in the Renfrewshire countryside.

Quarrier had long harboured the idea of training boys for the sea. When he was given £3,000 by the widow of a man called James Arthur, he decided to build a ship on land and name it after the benefactor. The ship was officially 'launched' on 1 March 1887 with the clear intention of training the best boys in the Home so that they would become 'working seamen for the mercantile navy.'[63]

Fully rigged with double topsail yards, the *James Arthur* was 120 ft long with a beam of 23 ft and a height of 9 ft between decks. She was fully equipped with stores and nautical gear, exactly as if she was bound for foreign shores. Accommodation was provided for thirty boys although the ship was actually large enough to take double that number. In addition to the *James Arthur*, two small boats were provided for use in the nearby River Gryffe and in these boys were taught how to row and sail. It was obviously an effective project as many Quarrier's boys passed from the homes into the Royal and Merchant Navies.

The *James Arthur* remained a feature of Quarrier's Homes for many years. When she was finally broken up in the second decade of the twentieth century it was only because managers of the home felt there was no longer any need for her service.

In March 1913, hundreds of spectators watched from the riverbanks as HMS *Stork* was towed to a permanent mooring off Upper Mall, Hammersmith, on

The rather battered hull of the *Implacable* shortly before she was towed out into the Channel and scuttled.

the Thames. Two years earlier the Admiralty had offered the old gunboat to the Kensington Branch of the Navy League for use as a training ship. There was, initially, some opposition to the ship being moored so close to residential properties. People in London knew of the *Cornwall, Exmouth* and the other training ships further downstream and feared that the presence of convict boys on the *Stork* would lead to the devaluation of property and a subsequent loss of amenities. In fact, the ship was to offer a very different kind of service.

This was a new scheme, its intention being to provide instruction and training to boys between the ages of twelve and seventeen who were already working but who wanted to join either the Royal Navy or the Royal Marines. 'Convict boys' were not in her remit. The trainees lived on board, paying for their board and lodge out of their wages, and went off to work each day at jobs in the city or the West End. They came back each night and from then on – and at weekends – came under naval control.

As well as passing on nautical skills, the routine of the *Stork* was designed to teach discipline, loyalty and observance of duty. Boys – or 'cadets' as they were called – had to be of good character and be physically fit. Having the ability to swim fifty yards, fully clothed, was one of the tests administered to all applicants. The upper deck of the ship was given over to teaching space while the stripped-out engine room was converted into a gymnasium. Cadets learned small boat work on one of the cutters attached to the *Stork*.

Hundreds of boys were prepared for careers at sea on board the *Stork*, the money to run her being provided by the Navy League and, later, by the British Legion. Fund raising activities and subscriptions also helped allay the costs of

A detailed view of the *Implacable*'s side.

Two training ships in one view, the *Cutty Sark* with, in the background, the *Foudroyant*, ex *Trincomalee*.

The original *Foudroyant*, Nelson's old flagship, is shown here off Blackpool just before she was wrecked.

keeping fifty boys on board. Preference was always given to the sons of ex-servicemen. The *Stork* remained in service throughout the Second World War but, eventually, dry rot in her timbers caused her to be condemned. She was towed away for breaking in 1950 and the scheme ended.

Two famous ships that also spent time as training vessels were the *Implacable* and the *Cutty Sark*. The *Implacable* was originally the French *Duguay Trouin*, a ship that escaped destruction at the Battle of Trafalgar only to be captured by Sir Richard Strachan two weeks later. After being renamed and serving in the Royal Navy for the duration of the Napoleonic Wars, she was laid up for many years before, in 1857, becoming a training hulk for boy entrants to the Navy. Stationed at Plymouth, she was moored bow to stern with the *Lion* and for nearly fifty years carried out this gruelling but necessary task. When the establishment of HMS *Ganges* centralised all Royal Navy boy entrant training, *Implacable* was left stranded and redundant.

In 1913, she was bought by a consortium of businessmen and moored in Falmouth Harbour as a private training ship. It was a simple process. Parents paid for their sons to spend time on board where they would be given a nautical education that, it was hoped, would help them in their future careers. She did not last long in this role and by the outbreak of war in 1939 the ship was almost at the end of her days. Nevertheless, with the sudden wartime influx of men into the Navy, every inch of space was needed and *Implacable* was requisitioned as an accommodation hulk for the duration of the war. By 1949 she was old and leaking with timbers rotting. Rather than hand her back to the French, she was towed out to sea and scuttled under the joint ensigns of France and Britain.

The *Cutty Sark* was also stationed at Falmouth. Famous as the finest of all the tea clippers, she was a beautiful ship but, by the end of the nineteenth century, her best days were behind her. Despite this, in 1895 she was sold to the Portuguese

The wreck of the *Foudroyant* – in the foreground is the Blackpool lifeboat attempting to take off the boys.

firm of J. A. Ferreira and sailed for another twenty-five years under the name *Ferreira* before being disabled in a gale off the Cape of Good Hope. In 1922 Captain Wilfred Dowman bought her from the Portuguese for the sum of £3,750. He had her towed to Falmouth, intending to use her as a training ship.

Restored to at least some of her former glory, the *Cutty Sark* lay at Falmouth until just before the Second World War, hundreds of young men and boys crowding her decks and rigging. Like the *Implacable* she was run as a profit making concern, Dowman having dreams of equipping her with a full suit of sails and sending her to sea with the trainees. The idea never got off the ground.

In 1936, after Dowman's death, his wife donated *Cutty Sark* to the Thames Nautical Training College and she was moored in the Thames, alongside the *Worcester* for several years. In 1949, the College turned her over to the National Maritime Museum and she was moved to Greenwich in time for the Festival of Britain in 1951. Land-locked, the *Cutty Sark* became a museum, being formally opened by Queen Elizabeth II on 25 June 1957.

The last of the voluntary or charity ships – and the only one still afloat – also had strong Falmouth connections. This was Joseph Cobb's *Foudroyant*. The original ship had been Nelson's flagship in the Mediterranean between 1799 and 1801, Nelson's daughter, Horatia, supposedly having been conceived in the stern cabin soon after Nelson and Emma Hamilton first met. Rescued from German breakers by Joseph Cobb, thousands of pounds were spent in restoring the ship. However, Cobb needed more, and in an effort to raise funds, in addition to taking money for training boys on board, he decided to sail her around the coast when the public would be bound to give money in order to see such an historic vessel.

Unfortunately, during this cruise the *Foudroyant* was wrecked at Blackpool on 16 June 1897 – the story of the wreck and rescue of the trainees is told elsewhere

The fatal damage to the *Foudroyant* can be clearly seen in this 1897 postcard view.

in this book – and Cobb died later the same year. Joseph Cobb's son Geoffrey decided to continue his father's work, but he needed a ship. He found one in the teak-built *Trincomalee*, launched at Bombay in 1817 and then engaged as Drill Ship at Southampton. The Admiralty was happy to sell her to Cobb and he took her to Cowes where she was stripped, coppered and converted, like her predecessor, to a training ship. As with the *Implacable* and *Cutty Sark*, the idea was that parents should pay Cobb a fixed sum for their children to be drilled in naval and nautical matters.

A five-year-long battle between Cobb and the snobbish Cowes Harbour Committee, which did not approve of a ship full of rowdy adolescents, finally saw him take his ship and moor her in the more receptive waters of Falmouth Harbour. There she was renamed *Foudroyant*. Having recently lost the *Ganges* training ship to Harwich, the people of Falmouth welcomed Cobb's new vessel with open arms.

They did not stay long, however. On 12 June 1904, the *Foudroyant* was towed to Milford Haven where she was moored between Pembroke Dock and Neyland. The trainees played a full part in the life of the small communities along the Haven. On 19 August 1904, for example, the *Foudroyant* boys competed in the Pembroke Dock Front Street Regatta while, on 31 August, the ship's band played at the Neyland Nursing Association Fete. There was almost a second disaster on 24 February 1905 when the ship dragged her anchors in a gale and had to be towed to safety by the Admiralty tug *Alligator*, from nearby Pembroke Dockyard.[64]

In the summer of 1905, Cobb moved the *Foudroyant* back to Falmouth where she was to stay for the next twenty-five years. Geoffrey Cobb was an irascible

The new *Foudroyant* is shown here during her move from Pembroke Dock to Portsmouth in 1932.

character, however, and in the 1930s a serious dispute arose between him and the Falmouth Harbour Board. The *Foudroyant* was held on a single mooring and, consequently, swung with the tide. As the harbour was becoming gradually more and more congested, the harbour board demanded she be moored fore and aft. Cobb refused and a long, protracted court case ensued. Eventually, Cobb took his ship away, moving her back to Pembroke Dock in September 1930. Thirty boys were then in training on board but many of the crew members, who had lived in Falmouth for years, resigned their positions rather than move to South Wales. The *Foudroyant* returned to the south coast in 1932, after the death of Geoffrey Cobb at Pembroke Dock Nursing Home the previous year. She was moored at Portsmouth where she remained for the next sixty years. Owned, now, by a charitable trust, she gradually became more of an outward-bound school as fewer and fewer opportunities presented themselves for careers at sea.

The role of voluntary or charity training ships is difficult to define. Unlike reformatory or industrial ships they did not have a specific task such as dealing with offenders or giving Mary Carpenter's 'perishing classes' a start in life. However, they did prepare boys for careers at sea, sometimes as a work of charity, sometimes because they were paid to do it. There is no doubt that they were very successful in their work and the affection in which most past pupils held them is proof positive, not only of the quality of their training, but also of the care and compassion the trainees received whilst living on board.

CHAPTER SIX
Officer Training Schools

The two officer training ships, *Conway* and *Worcester*, are perhaps the best known of all the wooden walls that were scattered around the coast of Britain during the nineteenth century. For many, they epitomised the whole nature of nautical training, proud old wooden warships without the stigma or taint of child criminals, poverty and neglect. Lying leisurely at anchor, hulls mirrored in the quiet waters of the Mersey and the Thames, they gave off an air of romantic charm but, at the same time, passers-by on the riverbank or trippers out on a Sunday afternoon cruise could gaze at them and know that the future of British seamanship was held in firm and steady hands.

Before the First World War there were only two ways for boys to become officers in the Merchant Navy. The first was to become an apprentice on board ship. Before the 1870 Education Act such apprenticeships often began as early as twelve or thirteen years – after 1870 the age was usually fifteen. Indentures were signed for four years, after which a boy could present himself for examination by the Board of Trade for his Second Mate's Certificate. The other way was to study at one of the two officer training ships and gain a firm grounding in nautical matters before embarking on a further period of training at sea.

These two ships might well have been designed for potential officers but conditions on board were only marginally better than on the reformatory or charity ships. A poem by John Masefield, entitled 'The *Conway*'s Word to the New-comer,' sums up the hardships and the attitude of staff and boys on both ships:

Here you will put off childhood and be free
Of England's oldest guild: here your right hand
Is the Ship's right, for service at command;
Your left may save your carcass from the sea.
And murmur afterwards, when you disband.
Here you will polish brass and scrub with sand,
And know as little leisure as the bee.[65]

The *Conway*, shown here off Rock Ferry on the Mersey.

Members of the Mercantile Marine Service Association first made the suggestion for a training ship on the Mersey in the early months of 1858. In true democratic fashion, a committee was appointed and began to meet to discuss options. The original idea was to train orphaned and destitute children of seamen as deckhands but, after much discussion, it was finally decided that something rather more significant was in order: 'The purpose of the Committee now became "to train boys to become officers in the Merchant Service;" it was, however, made a part of the plan that the orphans of deceased officers should be received on easier terms than others.'[66]

The sixth-rate man-of-war HMS *Conway* was offered by the Admiralty and quickly accepted by the committee. Liverpool ship owner John Clint went to Devonport to oversee operations while she was fitting out and remained there until the *Conway* was finally pronounced ready for removal on 6 January 1859. She duly arrived in the Mersey on 9 February and a few days later took up her moorings off the Rock Ferry Slip. She was equipped to take 120 boys and the money for this was raised by donations and subscriptions from Liverpool ship owners and other sailors and ship builders who were interested in the scheme.

The slightly larger HMS *Winchester* replaced the original vessel in 1861 although the name *Conway*, already established and recognised by ship owners and the general public, was retained. The ship had exclusive company for a while, Brunel's *Great Eastern* mooring abreast of her after one cruise to America. The side-wheel Cunard paddlers *Scotia* and *Persia* also moored close by on many occasions.

The early days were full of adventure. One morning, soon after the ship had begun work, the *Conway* found herself adrift, free of her moorings. A ferry

Another view of the *Conway*, this time with the cadets on the rigging and lined up along the deck.

steamer managed to get a line across and towed the ship to a safe position where the *Conway* was able to drop her anchor. New moorings were created and on lifting the old chain it was found that no fewer than fifteen anchors, each with an accompanying length of chain came up with it.

The first captain in charge was Charles Powell. He had been, for many years, commander of West Indian mail steamers and he was assisted by a chief officer, four seamen instructors, a carpenter, two stewards and two cooks. A headmaster, second master and two assistant masters provided education. The great advantage of such an organisational structure was that boys – who often went to sea at the age of thirteen and thus missed out on much of their formal education – could now combine academic and nautical study. As the ship took boys as young as twelve this was an important feature of the curriculum.

Shipping companies were soon indicating that, as far as the *Conway* was concerned, they would be happy to reduce the length of the Merchant Navy officers' apprenticeship. For young men who had spent time on board and had effectively passed out, they declared, this period could be cut from four to three years. In the early days, however, many boys came to the ship, stayed a term or two and then took up the usual apprenticeship at sea – in effect using the *Conway* for little more than sea practice. In 1861 the Board of Trade ruled that two years on the *Conway* would count as one spent at sea, thus formally shortening the apprenticeship period. This concession put an end to boys staying on board for only a few short months.

By 1863, there were 117 youngsters in training, a year later this figure had risen to 123 and life was rugged and hard. The upper deck had to be scrubbed

Above: The *Worcester* is shown here in a painting by marine artist W. L. Wylie – plenty of activity in this rather romanticised view.

Left: A cigarette card showing boys from the *Worcester* practising in their longboats for the annual *Conway–Worcester* Race.

Cadets on the *Worcester* practise with the sextant on this Senior Service cigarette card view.

THE THAMES NAUTICAL TRAINING COLLEGE.

H.M.S. "WORCESTER,"

OFF GREENHITHE, KENT.

ESTD.

1862

INCORP.

1893

H.M.S. "WORCESTER."

FOR the training of Youths intending to become Officers in the Mercantile Marine. Two years' training counts as one year's sea service for qualified cadets. Appointments granted by the Admiralty as Midshipmen in the Royal Navy and R.N.R., also by the India Office, in the Bengal Pilot Service, R.I.M., etc. A few Scholarships are also available, whilst Shipowners give preference to "Worcester" Cadets.

Over 3,000 "Worcester" Cadets have qualified as Officers in the Mercantile Marine.

For illustrated prospectus apply: *The Secretary,*
THAMES NAUTICAL TRAINING COLLEGE,
'Phone : *Royal* 3548. 72 MARK LANE, LONDON, E.C.3.

An early-twentieth-century advertisement for the *Worcester*.

ESTD.
1862.

INCORP.
1893.

H.M.S. "WORCESTER."

THAMES NAUTICAL TRAINING COLLEGE H.M.S. WORCESTER

OFF GREENHITHE, KENT.

President : Rear-Admiral H.R.H. The Prince of Wales, K.G., etc.

Chairman : Rt. Hon. The Earl of Inchcape, G.C.S.I., G.C.M.G., K.C.I.E.

Captain-Superintendent : Lt.-Comdr. G. C. Steele, V.C., R.N.

Primary object. The Training of Youths as Executive Officers for the Maritime Services. Combines special nautical and commercial subjects with PUBLIC SCHOOL EDUCATION. The training counts as one year's Sea service for certificated cadets. Appointments granted by the Admiralty in the R.N. and R.N.R. Ages 12-17. Moderate terms. Scholarships available from £100 to £50 p.a. For illustrated prospectus apply Secretary, Thames Nautical Training College, 72 Mark Lane, E.C.3.

According to this advert, the *Worcester* combined sea training with Public School Education.

Left: Moderate terms are offered on this advertisement for the *Worcester*.

Below: Sport was always important – this postcard view from 1935 shows *Worcester* boys playing rugby on the pitch alongside the ship.

A post-war shot, showing the old *Exmouth*, loaned to the Thames Nautical College after 1945 and renamed *Worcester*.

every day, regardless of the weather, this hated chore being carried out in bare feet. Boys were divided into starboard and port watches, one being engaged in formal education while the other took nautical instruction on the top deck. After dinner (always taken at twelve precisely) the watches changed around. Boys were given a month's leave at Christmas, another month in the summer, while shore leave would be granted to visit friends or relatives from noon on Saturday until Sunday evening, provided notes of invitation were presented to the staff. The ship was divided into numerous messes, usually of thirteen, ruled over with an iron fist by boy petty officers who were not averse to using the rope's end on the backs of anyone who did not give them immediate attention.

As might be expected on a ship full of adolescents, all working to a vigorous and hardy regime, a fair amount of bullying took place. New boys were particularly vulnerable targets. As one ex-*Conway* boy later wrote about his time on board in the late 1880s, 'I don't think I shall ever forget the stinging clout on my head I got on my first day; and all my toffee was taken from me. There was too much bullying, and small new chums were not looked after as they should have been. The result was that I lived to bully other small boys but, thank goodness, I was soon ashamed of myself.'[67]

Between 1890 and 1892 there was much discontent on the vessel with one or two attempts at mutiny and even some conspiracies to destroy ship's property. One of the most hated institutions on the *Conway* was an invention of Captain Miller who was in charge between 1881 and 1903. Every new boy was invited to become a member of 'the league', promising to avoid drinking, swearing and all forms of impurity. Those who were brave enough to refuse membership often felt themselves to be 'marked men'. There were distractions, however: 'The cook was known as 'Greasy Bill,' and the name fitted him. He volunteered to dive off the foreyard arm in the dog-watch if we could collect sufficient sixpences. We collected enough and Bill appeared to do his big dive. Meanwhile, the chief officer got to know of this and also appeared. Bill was sent back to his galley and all our sixpences were commandeered to buy brass-cleaning gear, so we not only lost the sight of Bill having a bath, which he badly needed, but our pocket money.'[68]

In 1876, the ninety-one-gun battleship, *Nile*, was acquired by the Mercantile Marine Service Association, the vessel being towed to the Mersey that July. She was a much larger vessel than her two predecessors and offered considerably more comfort to the boys. Her name was changed to *Conway*, boys hoisting everything out of the old ship – guns, masts, and yards – and storing them on the new vessel before going home for their summer holidays.

When they returned after their summer break boys found the new *Conway* almost ready for them. Paraffin lamps were now provided for lighting but as the flash point of the oil was very low there was a real risk of fire. The boys experimented with new fire extinguishers but were not very successful. They nearly set the ship alight before they were finally able to smother the flames with sand.

Two of the biggest taboos on the *Conway* were smoking and tattooing – at least as far as the officers were concerned. The boys took a rather different outlook on both of these forbidden fruits. As one trainee later said, 'I learned to smoke in less than a week, and had incredible designs done on my arm in Indian ink and vermilion. This was done by a mate lying flat in the fore-top, out of the officers' sight.'[69]

There was some limited contact between boys on the *Conway* and those on the nearby reformatory ships, *Akbar* and *Clarence*. Once the *Conway* boys were called on to help out when a fire broke out on the *Clarence*. Apparently the *Clarence* boys refused to man the pumps and, much to their disgust, the officer cadets witnessed quite a bit of brutal treatment by the officers on the reformatory ship. Boats from the *Conway* and *Akbar* used to meet at the Rock Ferry Slip when going ashore for stores. When their officer's back was turned the *Conway* lads would often slip a loaf of bread or a packet of sweets into the other boat.

Over the years there were many instances of the *Conway* being rammed, collided with or fouled by other ships dragging their anchors in the busy Mersey shipping lanes. One of the most notable incidents came in 1875 when the Liverpool guardship broke away from her moorings, crashed into the *Conway* and carried away a boat and other gear from the starboard side. In compensation the Royal Navy presented the ship with a new longboat and new running gear.

On 1 February 1885, the 2,000th trainee entered the ship and a year later 116 boys had the privilege of forming a guard of honour when Queen Victoria visited the Liverpool Exhibition. The Queen's Golden Jubilee was in 1887 and the *Conway* boys all took ship to Llandudno on board a steam tug to celebrate. There they went ashore and spent the day drinking lemonade and eating vast quantities of sticky buns.

On 26 April 1891, a young trainee was lost overboard for the first and only time in the ship's history. The boy was designated as a mizzen topman and was also a clever and versatile musician. He was on deck playing hide-and-seek one evening, in the interval between school and tea. Hide-and-seek on the upper deck was prohibited because it led people into potentially dangerous situations but it was very popular with all the boys, especially mizzen topmen who loved to outwit the petty officers. One boy was thought to have gone out onto one of the davits to hide just as the pipe went to call everyone in to tea – or 'stand by tables' as it was known. The boy was thought to have rushed to tea, missed his footing and gone overboard. His body was not found until many weeks later.

On discharge most *Conway* boys became deck officers in the Merchant Navy, as was always intended. Some went to the Royal Indian Marine and some to the Bengal Pilot Service. However, a limited number of the best and brightest trainees could be nominated for further officer training by the Royal Navy, firstly on the *Britannia* and then, when she was replaced, at Osborne and Dartmouth Colleges. Qualification was by an examination held at Osborne. After a visit from Winston Churchill in September 1912 the limit to the number of boys who could be nominated was removed. In 1913, the Osborne class on the *Conway* consisted of sixty-one boys out of a total number of 190 on the books.

Amongst well-known *Conway* boys was Matthew Webb, the first man to swim the English Channel, later drowned trying to swim across Niagara Falls. Strangely, he was not considered a great swimmer while on board, being easily beaten in any race, but he did have great staying power and could swim for hours without putting his feet down. The poet John Masefield, famous for his poem 'Sea Fever', was another trainee. He also wrote the classic account of the ship's early days and, like most *Conway* boys, remained inordinately proud of the vessel and his time on board.

The *Conway* remained on station on the Mersey until the dark days of the Second World War. Then, in 1941, with the German bombing offensive at full height, the Mercantile Marine Service Association decided that the ship would be safer away from Liverpool and its valuable docks. As a result she was moved to the Menai Straits, a station that she maintained right to the end.

The Thames Nautical Training College, better known simply as HMS *Worcester*, was the brainchild of the merchant William Munton Bullivant and the Blackwall ship builder, Richard Green. They were concerned about the character and training of young Merchant Navy officers on board ship: 'Many of the captains and mates under whom they served were . . . brutal and ignorant to a degree. These were conditions not calculated to breed the best type of sailor and future officer. There was the need for special training, if vessels were to be supplied with a more suitable type.'[70]

Bullivant knew of the work of the *Conway* on the Mersey and thought that the Thames should also have the services of an officer training ship. At a meeting in his offices on 26 September 1861 a committee was formed and it was resolved to establish such a vessel, the original name for the institution being The Thames Marine Officers' Training Ship. Subscriptions soon came flooding in from ship owners, traders and sailors, and the Admiralty – at first not interested – soon

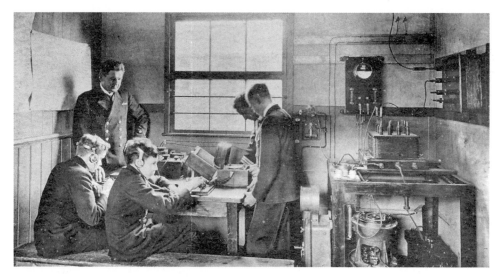

The Wireless Room at Pangbourne College.

began to see some value in the scheme. On 7 October 1861, they agreed to loan HMS *Worcester*, a fifty-gun frigate, then lying off Sheerness. Brought to Blackwall Reach, she was handed over to the committee on 29 May 1862. Initially moored at Erith, the first commander was Capt J. F. Trivett and when the college first opened on 4 August 1862 it had just fourteen students. Four months later there were twenty-seven on board, and by June 1864 the number stood at eighty-five.

Boy entrants to the ship were to be aged between twelve and fifteen years old, no boy to remain on board once he reached the age of seventeen. The original fees were set at thirty-five guineas per annum, with a further charge of five guineas for uniform and two guineas for medical attention and washing. There were to be two terms a year and preference was given to the sons of officers in the Merchant Navy. The nautical curriculum included basics such as knotting and splicing but went on to include study of navigation and nautical astronomy. Chart drawing, trigonometry, mechanics, marine surveying and French were also studied. New subjects were added to the curriculum from time to time, to take account of modern developments. A radio branch, for example, was established just before the First World War.[71]

As with the *Conway*, the Board of Trade quickly agreed that two years training on the *Worcester* could reduce a boy's apprenticeship by a full year. The Admiralty also encouraged boys to qualify themselves for cadetship in the Royal Navy, the first naval cadetship being granted in April 1868. Commissions were also granted in the Royal Naval Reserve, the first thirteen boys being appointed in July 1873. It made sense to have qualified and experienced sailors, already working at sea, available to be called into the Royal Navy should the need arise, and both the *Worcester* and the *Conway* provided manpower for the RNR.

In its early days the *Worcester* lived something of a nomadic existence. In July 1869 she was moved from Erith, where the moorings were considered unhealthy,

In the Seamanship Room boys learned the intricacies of their future profession under the guidance of experts.

to Southend. However, it was a very exposed mooring and frequent bad weather off the Essex seaside town constantly made the boys seasick. In some bad storms it was impossible to get stores on board. So the committee decided to move the ship to Greenhithe. To celebrate the occasion the boys fired a salute from the *Worcester*'s guns – gunnery then being considered an important part of every sailor's training – with the result that many of the windows in the Greenhithe cottages were promptly shattered.

By 1875, there were so many boys in training on board that the old *Worcester* was considered too small. The screw line-of-battleship *Frederick William* was duly loaned by the Admiralty and took up position at Greenhithe before being renamed *Worcester* – like the *Conway* her name was already well-known in all shipping circles. At the same time, the institution formally adopted the name Thames Nautical Training College, HMS *Worcester*. When Capt David Wilson-Barker became Commander in February 1877 it was a unique moment – Wilson-Barker had himself been a cadet on the *Worcester*.

The aim of all cadets was to gain a *Worcester* Board of Trade certificate and then find a position with one of the main shipping companies. These shipping companies quickly assessed the worth of the training and were always keen to plunder the *Worcester* lists for suitable candidates for apprenticeships. In May 1907 the P & O Company even inaugurated a scholarship on board. P & O would pay half the fees for suitable boys, parents the other half. In January 1926, the various city guilds of London began granting scholarships to the *Worcester*. So desirable were places on board that in May 1928 it was decided that an entrance exam was now required for anyone wanting a place on the ship.

The yacht *St George*, used by Pangbourne for five voyages in the 1920s.

Good conduct badges were awarded to suitable boys in their fourth term on board but only if they had reached the second section in seamanship. Holders of these badges enjoyed certain privileges, such as being able to stay up after the usual time for 'turning in' – 8.30 in the winter, 9.30 in summer.

The so-called 'cadet captains' were chosen from the holders of good conduct badges. First class captains had charge of either the forecastle, fore, main mizzen or after-guard tops while second class captains took charge of the band, the games room, sports field and working parties on the Abbey Estate. Ingress Abbey Estate had been acquired in 1920, making sports fields, changing rooms and a sanatorium suddenly available. An indoor pool in the old abbey building replaced the old canvas bath that had been located under the bows of the ship since 1863.

Examinations were held each year, each boy hopefully progressing towards his Worcester Board of Trade Certificate. A wide range of topics was covered, including English, Maths, Scripture, Geography and nautical subjects. Questions varied between simple and complex, often being geared towards the future careers of the boys. In Geography, for example, they would be asked not just about the capitals or rivers of certain countries but would also be posed questions like this: 'In coasting from Aberdeen to London what headlands, towns, rivers and bays would be passed? Where would you find good anchorage en route?'

Discipline on board the *Worcester* was well managed and never unduly repressive. There was an unofficial system of 'fagging' in existence where all boys whose stay was under four terms fagged for the seniors and a number of initiation ceremonies were also held for new boys – a 'crossing the line' ceremony and having to sing before the senior boys being just two of them. Old hands – anyone in their third or fourth term – were allowed to have pockets in their trousers and to wear their caps slack or perched on the back of their heads.

There were many famous *Worcester* boys, none more so than Adml Togo, victorious Japanese admiral at the Battle of Tsu-Shima in 1905 when the Russian fleet was totally destroyed. He was clearly fond of his old training ship, even though he had lied about his age – reducing it by almost ten years – to gain admission. He returned to visit the ship in 1911 and wrote a letter to all *Worcester* boys: 'I am one of the Old Boys of the Worcester who learnt to be sailors more than thirty years ago on this very ship, as you are doing now. Today I am so much pleased to meet you on board our beloved ship. Your cheerful and vigorous appearances make me firmly believe in your bright future.'[72]

When Robert Falcon Scott went on his last and fatal expedition to Antarctica in 1912, two *Worcester* boys went with him. Lieutenant (later Admiral) Teddy Evans, the second-in-command, returned to write a best-selling book about the trip. He also gained fame as 'Evans of the Broke', the destroyer he commanded in the Dover Patrol during the First World War. The other *Worcester* boy on the expedition was Lt H. R. Bowers who perished with Scott on their return trip from the South Pole.

During the Second World War, with London being nightly ravaged by enemy bombers, the college was evacuated to Foots Cray Place, near Sidcup. The *Worcester* herself was requisitioned by the Royal Navy and used as a training base. By now, however, the ship was old and dilapidated and the presence of heavy-footed recruits clomping around the decks certainly did not help. A mixture of good luck and the use of a large salvage pump that worked virtually around the clock, managed to keep her afloat.

After the war the *Worcester* was handed back to the college but the ship was clearly of little use. The college was saved by the donation of the industrial training ship, *Exmouth*, now back from duties in Scapa Flow and, for a while, things carried on as normal. There was a great demand for places in the 1940s and 1950s, before the decline in British shipping set in during the 1960s. And for this brief period the fortunes of the college shone like a blazing star. By 1968, however, there was just no reason for continued existence and the college closed. The *Worcester* was towed away and the Ingress abbey estate was handed over to create the Merchant Navy College. Unfortunately, this establishment lasted only twenty years and the area has now become a housing estate.

One of the best-known features of the *Conway* and *Worcester* was the annual rowing contest between the two ships. The first race was rowed on 5 June 1890, in response to a challenge from the *Conway* boys. The race was won by the *Worcester* over a course of 2 miles and 200 yards. The following year the *Conway* proved victorious. Races took place on the Thames and Mersey alternately and during the 1894 race on the Thames, staging alongside the *Worcester* collapsed, pitching a dozen or so spectators into a choppy river. Fortunately all of the wet and frightened spectators were rescued.

Ordinary ships' boats were used for the races and the staff of the two ships trained the crews, although there were occasionally complaints about outside

Pangbourne boys at play – note the boy on the left. As well as playing billiards he is also clearly ready to take to the rugby field.

coaches being brought in to help. The races were discontinued at the request of the *Worcester* after 1906 when *Conway* claimed victory and, therefore, held on to the cup and shield.

The contests were revived in 1929, the *Worcester* quickly gaining the upper hand in the first race and holding it for the rest of the 1930s. In all the meetings there was only one dead-heat, that of 1905, when bad style and arguments in the *Conway* boat clearly lost them the advantage.

The *Conway* and *Worcester* were not the only training schools for officers, although it was nearly twenty years into the twentieth century before they were joined by the third such establishment. Pangbourne College was a land-based school situated on the upper reaches of the Thames in Berkshire, an establishment that owed its existence to the indomitable figure of Thomas Lane Devitt of the Devitt & Moore shipping line.

Devitt had long held a desire to found a nautical college, a place that would augment his sea-going training ships like the *Port Jackson* and *Macquarie*. After much consideration and searching he discovered an appropriate site, the Clayesmore Estate at Pangbourne, in November 1916. He returned to his board of directors and broke the news to them. He then promptly sold off the *Port Jackson* and bought the estate with the proceeds. The Board of Trade and the Admiralty, both desperate to build up manpower in the light of Germany's recent declaration of unrestricted submarine warfare and fuelled by the nightmare vision of continual war losses, backed him in his plans. Devitt poured money and energy into the new project: 'great progress was made in the plans for adapting the newly acquired building at Pangbourne and for drawing up the curriculum of the College, the fullest care being taken to ensure that as much general education as possible should be given in conjunction with the necessary amount of technical instruction to those boys who wished to enter the Merchant Service.'[73]

The first twenty-five cadets were admitted on 1 September 1917, Capt W. H. F. Montanaro being the first captain superintendent. Youngsters were admitted between the ages of thirteen and fourteen and were expected to spend four terms at the college. The year was divided into two terms, September to December, January to July, with a short break at Easter. As well as courses in practical seamanship boys studied trigonometry, navigation, engineering and all of the other necessary subjects to make them competent officers in the Merchant Marine. The original plan was for boys to follow a period at Pangbourne with a further course of studies on board ship, with Devitt & Moore's ocean training ships, but in 1918 the *Medway*, last of these sail training ships, was requisitioned by the Ministry of Shipping.

The auxiliary yacht, *St George*, was purchased as a replacement but the cost of purchase and fitting out was prohibitive in the immediate post war years. Nevertheless, it was something Devitt felt he had to do as he had made a commitment and had an obligation to the parents of boys already in training. The tiny ship made five voyages in all, using Plymouth as her home base, before she was laid up and sold in May 1921.

Despite this setback, the college grew quickly. In December 1919 there were 193 cadets in residence but the depression was beginning to hit Devitt & Moore, like all shipping companies, quite badly. Pangbourne was, quite simply, haemorrhaging money. Although it had been decided to increase fees to £160 a year, this did not apply to existing cadets and so it was 1923 before the college even began to look like breaking even. It was a difficult time but the work continued and a regular stream of cadets passed out into the Merchant and Royal Navies. By 1930 the College was well established, 61 per cent of cadets entering the Merchant Navy on completion of their course. The others went to the Royal Air Force, the Royal Navy and the Army, and 24 per cent entered civilian life.[74]

After the death of Thomas Devitt in 1923, his son, Philip, took over the reins of the shipping company and of Pangbourne. He ran them both for several years but, in order to safeguard the college for future generations, in 1931 he decided to set up a board of governors and to create a private company that would run Pangbourne as a non-profit making concern.

With the decline of the British shipping industry after the Second World War it was clear that, if Pangbourne were to survive it would have to broaden its outlook and its aims. This it managed to do quite successfully. The college still exists, run these days as a co-educational public school and not as a purely nautical concern. Some nautical connections remain, however, and the school is renowned as one of the best rowing academies in the country.

Formal officer training for the Merchant Navy for boys on ships like *Conway* and *Worcester* and in places like Pangbourne is now largely a thing of the past. Yet there is still officer training available for those who want and need it. These days it comes at university level and students have to be sponsored by shipping lines or companies. Courses tend to consist of a combination of theoretical study and experiential learning at sea. Those interested in becoming navigating officers may follow courses at places like the Fleetwood Nautical Campus (in conjunction with Liverpool John Moore's University), Glasgow College of Nautical Studies, Plymouth University or Warsash Maritime Academy. Warsash, in conjunction with Southampton Solent University, also offers courses for engineering officers, as do the Glasgow College of Nautical Studies, South Tyneside College and Greenwich University.

The history of specific officer training for the Merchant Navy lives on and, when people talk of the training ships, it is invariably vessels like the *Conway* and *Worcester* that they are recalling. They were a unique and fascinating concept and there is no doubt that the world will never see their like again.

CHAPTER SEVEN
Stone Frigates – Land-based Nautical Schools

By the beginning of the twentieth century, people were already beginning to wonder about the nature of nautical training. Would it be better, they asked, if such training was offered on land rather than afloat? There was no clear or easy answer and, as we have seen, no real decision was taken until the destruction of the *Warspite* in 1918 finally made educationalists and philanthropists bite the bullet.

Many charities had toyed with the idea of nautical training during the nineteenth century, not least the renowned Barnardo organisation. Thomas Barnardo himself had long held the desire to create such an establishment and when, in the 1890s, he saw the old county school site at Elmham in Norfolk he marked it down as an almost perfect location. At the time, however, he could not afford the purchase price and so it was not until June 1901 that Edmund Hannay Watts, senior partner in Watts, Watts & Co. shipping line, bought the site and presented the deeds to Barnardo's. Dr Barnardo spent much of the last five years of his life planning his new venture.

New building and repair work cost well over £10,000 and it was not until April 1903 that the first thirty boys – orphans, waifs and strays, as they were described – moved into the new Watts Naval Training School. Even then the building work was not finished and for the first few months boys and staff went about their business with the monotonous grind of saws and hammers going on all around them. Barnardo did not live to see the formal opening of his new school in April 1906 but by then the place was fully staffed and equipped for 320 boys.

The Mission to Deep Sea Fishermen loaned a tender, the *Cholmondeley*, to Watts School and this gave students the chance to cruise along the east coast in summer months. Another vessel, the rather bigger ninety-four-ton ketch, *G. L. Munro*, was used to provide sea training.

Education was given, full-time, until boys reached the age of fourteen but after that their programme of training was slanted deliberately towards nautical instruction. The school was organised into six divisions and boys slept in one of eleven dormitories, all of which were named after famous admirals. All students went barefoot, even while playing football and cricket.[75]

The Watts Naval Training School, Barnardo's first nautical school at North Elmham in Norfolk.

The day at Watts began about 5.45 a.m. Precisely fourteen minutes later, not a second longer or shorter, the bugler sounded 'Still' and all boys knelt by their beds in silent prayer – or, more probably, in anticipation of breakfast! 'Clean Ship' followed, then a quick cross-country run or a series of physical exercises. Breakfast was taken at 7 a.m. More jobs followed and then came assembly beneath the mast. School lasted most of the day, finishing promptly at 5 p.m. After a brief period of leisure – not too much as idleness was dangerous and therefore not to be encouraged – supper was at 7 p.m. This usually consisted of a mug of cocoa and a handful of broken biscuits. At bedtime 'each boy was given a dessertspoonful of salt in his cupped hands as one by one the 300 boys went to the troughs with cold water taps, to clean their teeth with salt and gargle with salt water. Then, boys lined up for inspection, baring their teeth in front of the duty officer'[76].

During the 1920s, a boating centre for the school was established on the Norfolk Broads. Here, using two cutters, a whaler and a skiff, boys were taken through a rigorous programme of sailing and oarsmanship. This was felt to be far more effective than going to sea on the *G. L. Munro* where, in reality, they learned little more than how to be seasick.

As the requirements of the Royal and, to a lesser extent, the Merchant Navies changed, the curriculum at Watts changed with them. Once it became clear that wireless operators were an essential commodity at sea, the school created a wireless class and by 1932 there were ten old Watts boys serving as wireless operators in the Merchant Marine.

Even at night the naval routine was continued. All night groups of boys stood watch, relieving each other every couple of hours, taking it turn and turn about to get used to this element of life on board ship. Like most nautical schools, Watts had

Boys of the Watts School pose with guns and limber in front of the ketch *G. L. Munro*, on which they used to take summer cruises.

an excellent band, playing marches and hornpipes whenever required. Many of the boys consequently found themselves in the Naval School of Music at Eastney.

Watts also ran an advanced class where candidates for the Admiralty gratuity, awarded to each boy who joined the Royal Navy, could be coached and groomed. Advanced class boys from Watts were given six months seniority to those who entered the Navy by the ordinary routes. The success of the school was easily monitored, as these figures from the Barnardo's organisation regarding leavers for the years 1928 to 1933 clearly show:

Destination	1928	1929	1930	1931	1932	1933
Royal Navy	35	37	15	29	32	26
Merchant Navy	6	6	11	2	5	4
Military Bands	2	5	10	18	17	17
Emigrated	5	3	11	12	4	–
Shore situations	18	22	31	22	11	30
Totals	66	73	78	83	69	30
Admiralty gratuity	12	8	3	10	12	7

(figures from the Barnardo's organisation)

Discipline at Watts was undoubtedly hard, six cuts with the cane being a standard punishment for even minor offences and rigorous control was maintained over the lives of the boys. A Minute from the Barnardo Council for July 1924 noted that students had often returned from leave with relatives and family with 'Bolshevik or

Communist ideas'. As a result a resolution was passed prohibiting all youngsters from going home for Christmas. The various schools and homes of the organisation, it was felt, were well enough equipped to give the boys a good time – certainly a high-handed approach but one that should be placed in the context of the time.[77]

The Watts School trained its boys primarily for the Royal Navy. Some boys did enter the Merchant Navy but for all Watts boys the 'Senior Service' was their prime aim. In an attempt to offer a similar service for the Merchant Marine, in 1919 Barnardo's founded the Russell-Cotes Nautical School for Merchant Seamen. Named after the donors of the land, Sir Merton and Lesley Russell-Cotes, the school was not run on quite the same rigid and highly disciplined lines as Watts. Situated in 34 acres of open ground at Parkstone in Dorset, to the west of Bournemouth, it was agreeably close to the sea. Boys lived in cottages on the estate, rather than dormitories, and punishments were altogether more humane. They were treated more as necessary corrections than acts of officially approved brutality.

On arrival at school each boy was given 1,000 marks. From then on everything he did, good, bad or indifferent, added to or subtracted from the original marks. If a boy was able to increase his total to 1,500 he earned a red star; 1,750 meant a silver star and 2,000 marks earned him a gold star. Privileges were granted to boys according to the number of stars they held. Barnardo's was clear; the organisation at Russell-Cotes was intended to move away from the traditional, Victorian concept of handing out charity to needy cases: 'In an elaborate publicity pamphlet published in 1919, Barnardo's described the new venture as philanthropic patriotism. "Surely nothing could be further from the old and hateful system of "charity doles" than this new scheme for making the poorest child a self-respecting and honourable citizen, a credit to his country and part of the bulwark of England." Their publicity reflected a new language of respect for the indigent child.'[78]

It was not just publicity. Once, when a boy robbed a bird's nest, the captain superintendent took the boy to his locker and confiscated his most prized possession for a brief period. He made his point. The school was less than half the size of Watts but it proved highly successful in placing boys into positions at sea. In the 1920s and '30s, for example, many Russell-Cotes boys were employed as stewards on the prestigious Union Castle Line. The involvement of Union Castle was a significant one, the company actually sponsoring many of the boys at the school.

One of the features of the Russell-Coates Nautical School was the number of rooms set aside for use by old boys when they returned to the school on leave. Such visits enabled the staff to monitor the development of boys who had left and gone to sea. They also provided a great stimulus to the boys in training, ex-pupils bringing back stories of adventure and of fantastic countries visited.

In the centre of a 'playground' just outside the school stood a mock up of a ship's bridge. 20 ft high, the bridge had a dual role. Here, boys learned signalling but also, on one side that had been smoothed over, ropes were slung so that they could practise climbing up the sheer, smooth side of a ship. Semaphore lessons were also given on the bridge and, using a large mast alongside, the boys were

A group of boys from Watts, all of who went on to serve in the Canadian Navy during the First World War.

Watts School during the hard winter of 1928.

John and Gladys Gibbs, founders of the NCH Training School, outside Buckingham Palace, prior to his award of the DSO.

The mast at the Gibbs Home – the view from the top was stunning as the mast stood on the edge of a 150-foot cliff!

Boys of the Gibbs Home prepare to take part in a town carnival.

instructed in the art of rocket rescue life-saving, one party of shipwrecked trainees being rescued by another party detailed off as the Rocket Crew.

In 1926, elementary education for boys aged ten to fourteen at the school was taken over by Poole Education Committee, thus ensuring quality schooling at a very impressionable age. Boys could join the nautical classes when they attained the age of fourteen and then spend a year or eighteen months in nautical training. Most of them left at about fifteen and a half, almost all leavers electing for careers at sea.

After the end of the Second World War the number of boys wanting to go to sea began to fall as the worldwide depression in the shipping industry started to bite. In 1949, Watts School was closed and the two Barnardo's nautical schools amalgamated on the Parkstone site. The new establishment was known as the Parkstone Sea Training School. It was a losing battle, however. During the 1950s and '60s less than half the leavers actually took to the sea and the school lacked the modern educational facilities needed to survive. Consequently, Parkstone Sea Training School closed its doors for the last time in the summer of 1964.

The National Children's Homes and Orphanages (now called Action for Children) was something of a rival to Barnardo's – if such a word can be used in relation to child-care and education. However, it too provided nautical training for some of its boys. Founded in 1869 by the Rev. Thomas Bowman Stephenson, the Methodist-based charity soon owned a large number of homes for destitute and orphaned children. Like Barnardo, Stephenson cherished the notion of providing a training ship, even going so far as to form a committee and, in the early 1890s, hold an open meeting to discuss the matter at the Mansion House in London. Money was raised and the Admiralty promised a ship but the National

The Duke of York, later King George VI, formally opens the school and inspects the trainees – Lt Commander Carr accompanies him down the line of waiting boys.

Children's Homes decided it would be too expensive a project and, reluctantly, the idea was dropped.

In September 1917, with the First World War at its height, Major John Angel Gibbs, from one of the leading ship-owning families in South Wales, was killed while leading his men in an attack on the Menin Road. For several years Gibbs and his wife had been interested in helping needy children and now Gladys Gibbs conceived a plan that would not only provide a fitting memorial for her husband but would also put some of their long-held plans into practice.

For £5,000 she bought the large, disused Penarth Hotel from the Taff Vale Railway Company and presented it to the National Children's Homes, on the condition that it should be used as a nautical training school. Cardiff had lost its industrial school, *Havannah*, some years before, but it was still an important port and the NCH accepted Mrs Gibbs' offer with alacrity. Despite some difficulty finding fixtures and fittings in these wartime years, the work of converting the place into a home and a school was effectively carried out and the Gibbs Home opened for business in late 1918.

Situated high up on the cliff overlooking both Cardiff and Penarth Docks, the new school was in an ideal position. Its development coincided with the general move away from ship-based training, although, being within a stones throw of the Severn Estuary and the Bristol Channel, there was always going to be the opportunity for practical training.

More importantly, because of the Gibbs connections, once boys had finished their training they could easily be found berths on ships of the Gibbs, Morel or Reardon Smith lines, all of which sailed their vessels out of Cardiff Docks. It was very much

NATIONAL CHILDREN'S HOME
AND ORPHANAGE

Established 1869   (Founded by Dr. Stephenson)

LUNCHEON

AT THE

J. A. GIBBS HOME, PENARTH

on the occasion of the Visit of Inspection

BY

HIS ROYAL HIGHNESS

THE DUKE OF YORK

WEDNESDAY, 27TH JULY, 1921

———

CHAIRMAN: COL. AND ALD.

Sir Charles Cheers Wakefield

BART., C.B.E.

The Luncheon Menu for the Duke's visit to
the Gibbs Home in July 1921.

Lieutenant Commander James Hugh
Turner, who became Governor of the Gibbs
Home in 1923, seen here in dress uniform.

a case of combining philanthropy with hard-headed pragmatism – the boys needed careers, the shipping companies needed sailors. Initially, at least, it was decided that preference would be given to children whose fathers had been killed in the war, thereby continuing the nineteenth-century ideal of giving children a chance in life rather than see them, through no real fault of their own, become a drain on society.

The old hotel was equipped as dormitory and group rooms while the nautical school was established in the old coach-house and stable block alongside. The first boy, Reginald Jones, was admitted on 24 October 1918 and within twenty-four hours he had been confined to bed with a temperature of 103 degrees. Audrey Bashford, a tiny seven-year-old whose father had been killed by the propeller of a flying machine, joined him in the sick bay the next day. The two brothers, Harold and Leslie Woodhouse were also amongst the first admissions. Harold went on to take a degree at Cardiff, became a Wrangler at Cambridge and sadly died while piloting a Lancaster bomber over Germany in 1943. Leslie joined the Royal Navy in 1925 and in 1931 was commissioned from the lower deck, a rare achievement in those days.[79]

Before long it was not just war orphans who were being catered for. Edwin Meak's placement was partially funded by the Titanic Relief Fund as his mother had been drowned when the *White Star* liner sank in 1912. Many youngsters from other NCH branches, boys who had expressed an interest in the sea, were also soon being transferred into the Gibbs Home.

Unusually, the first officer in charge was a woman, Sister Ella Curnock, and all of the early staff were members of the Methodist Sisterhood. Such early elementary training and sea work as the home provided came from these doughty ladies, all of whom were addressed by the boys as 'Sir' – a derivation of 'Stir' which, in its turn, came from the word 'Sister'. The home was formally opened by the Duke of York on 27 July 1921. After inspecting the boys and then taking lunch in the school dining-hall – the fare was hardly what the boys normally received – the formal proceedings were concluded with speeches. In his address the Duke (later King George VI) was clear about the value of establishments such as the Gibbs Home and of the way the school would help preserve the memory of John Angel Gibbs: 'I can think of no finer way of perpetuating his memory than the foundation of this Home, and so helping on the Empire in whose service he gave his life, by assisting to train some of its citizens in the essential calling of the sea.'[80]

The idea of the sisters training boys was only a temporary one and soon Lt Cdr F. P. Carr was appointed as nautical instructor. In 1923 Lt Cdr James Hugh Turner arrived to take charge of the home. Commissioned from the lower deck, Turner had served on the monitors *Terror* and *Marshal Soult* during the war years, but his best work was undoubtedly as superintendent and, later, governor of the NCH Gibbs Home.

Turner soon had over 100 boys under his caring and capable wing. During the day boys attended Albert Road School in Penarth – their nautical training took place in the evenings or at weekends or, more usually, once they had reached school-leaving age and elected to stay on for a further year in order to further their nautical studies. The home/school kept a rowing boat and sailing craft in a

HMS *Mal de Mer*, the seasickness machine at the Gibbs Home. Note the boy at the front of the device; he is carefully rocking the platform to simulate movement at sea.

boatshed near to Penarth Docks but one of its most interesting training devices was HMS *Mal de Mer*, a rolling platform designed by Lt Cdr Carr. Its purpose was two-fold: to teach youngsters to steer a ship whilst being thrown from side to side and to help them cope with the effects of seasickness.

As with most nautical schools tragedy was invariably hovering in the wings. The school logbook for 26 March 1924 records that Reginald Spriggs was killed when 'he fell under the keel of the boat, the stern post crushing his stomach and rupturing his liver. He passed away of an internal haemorrhage about 10.50am, 25 to 30 minutes after the accident.'[81]

Another death occurred on 1 October 1931 when Ronald Wixey, a thirteen-year-old boy then in training, fell over the cliffs whilst trying to recover the handkerchief of another boy. The handkerchief had been lost while being used as a sling to propel stones out over the cliff and onto the beach below. Wixey offered to get the handkerchief for the payment of half a penny each week out of the boy's pocket money. He was discovered to be absent from his bed after 'Lights Out' and when a rope was found to be missing from the school it was clear what he intended. Unfortunately the rope came loose and Ronald Wixey fell over a hundred feet to the beach below. He died just as the rescue party discovered him.

The Methodist sisters continued to work as housemothers at the Gibbs Home for many years, offering a caring hand and a degree of compassion that were almost unknown in many of the other schools. Even so, many of the boys had mixed feelings about the treatment they received: 'I regret that I cannot lend any support

Boys repairing small boats at the Prince of Wales Sea Training Hostel in Limehouse, London – only later was the name of the establishment changed from Hostel to School.

to the suggestion that the NCH was, during the years I was at the Gibbs Home, in the avant garde of child care as practically all my recollections of the place are unpleasant. The main source of pleasure was the company of all the other boys.'[82]

Other youngsters remembered their old training establishment with rather more pleasure, even if the delights and enjoyment were not quite what the undoubtedly harassed sisters always had in mind: 'After the bugle called 'lights out,' maybe I would go on talking and Sister Nora would tell me to stand at a window at the end of the corridor. I wonder whether she knew that I really enjoyed my punishment? Looking over the lights of Cardiff Docks and watching the passing ships, plenty of them in those days, going up and down the Bristol Channel.'[83]

Many of the Gibbs Home boys went on to successful careers at sea. Stanley Greenway, for example, the third boy admitted to the home, rose to become captain of several different merchant ships. Another ex-pupil was Stanley Unwin who served as a radio operator, then gave up the sea and became famous as an actor and comedian with his wonderful mispronunciations and mangling of the English language. Did he, perhaps, learn this trick at the Gibbs Home?

With the demand for sailors dropping away because of the worldwide depression of the 1920s and '30s, the National Children's Homes began to look carefully at the use and value of the Gibbs Home. The shipping industry might be in decline but delinquency figures were rising, right across the country. When the organisation was approached by the Home Office with a view to creating one of the new approved schools that had replaced reformatories (as per the terms of the 1933 Children and Young Persons Act) its senior officials made a carefully considered

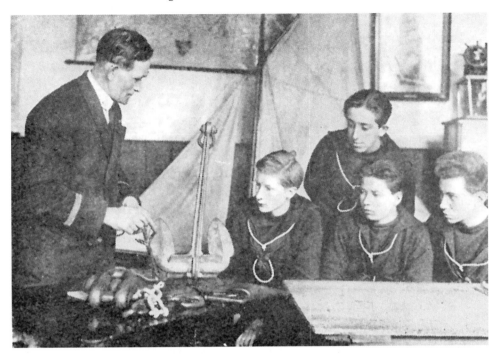

Instruction in the use and type of anchors used at sea for the boys of the Prince of Wales Hostel.

decision. The Gibbs Home would cease to function as a nautical training school and would convert into an approved school. This duly took place in 1936. Known now as Headlands School, the establishment is still running, these days functioning as a special school for children with significant social, emotional and educational problems. It is one of just a handful of ex-nautical schools still in existence.

Cardiff, of course, retained its connection with nautical training long after the Gibbs Home changed its function. In 1921 the Reardon Smith College was opened in the city, offering training to apprentices, principally young men who had signed indentures to the shipping line of the same name. The College ran for many years from its base at Fairwater, throughout the war years and into the 1950s and 60s before amalgamating with a local Technical College in 1976.

There were many other land-based schools that operated with considerable degrees of success over the years, far too many to mention or describe. Some, however, are worthy of note as they became renowned with seafarers all across the world. For example, the Lancashire and National Sea Training Hostel for Boys was established in 1896 as the Liverpool Branch of the Navy League. Situated in Withens Lane in Wallasey, for a brief period between 1907 and 1908 the establishment was called The Lancashire (Navy League) Home for Poor Boys. In 1916 the name was changed again, this time to the Lancashire and National Sea Training Home for Boys, the name that it retained until 1945 when the institution merged with the training ship *Indefatigable*, the new establishment being called The Indefatigable and National Sea Training School for Boys.

Located, in later years, at Liscard, Cheshire, the home had a staff of twelve and was able to cater for up to 140 trainees. It took poor boys of good character between the ages of thirteen and fifteen, nearly 80 per cent of them going to sea with the Merchant Navy, 10 per cent with the Royal Navy. The home received an education grant and a certificate from local government enabled them to take workhouse boys at a charge of £18.50 per annum. Interestingly, boys were indentured to the home for a period of three years, during which time, at the end of each voyage, they returned to the home where they remained until they had signed on for another ship – an early and rare example of positive 'after-care.'

The Prince of Wales Sea Training School was founded in the Limehouse area of London in 1920, shortly after training ships had ceased to be the flavour of the month. Originally called the Prince of Wales Sea Training Hostel, the school was originally designated to take fifty students. The first commanding officer was not a sailor but an Army man, Mr Godfrey E. Halsey. He ran the school from its inception until 1937.

Due to the need to keep boys safe from the German bombing raids the school moved to Ingham in Norfolk in 1940. Then, renamed the Prince of Wales Sea Training School, it moved to Dover in 1953. Before the establishment finally closed its doors in 1975 over 5,000 boys – usually aged between fifteen and seventeen – had passed through its portals. Most of the boys were trained as deck ratings, one sad fact being that eighty-five ex-Prince of Wales boys lost their lives at sea during the Second World War.

The last chief officer of the school was Cdr Joseph George Hadley who was in post between 1953, when the establishment moved to Dover, and 1976, the year after it closed. He had trained at the Prince of Wales Sea Training School as a boy and later, when he came ashore, became chief instructor.

The Royal Merchant Seamen's Orphanage at Snaresbrook was originally set up in 1827 to provide care and education for the orphan children of Merchant Seamen. After the First World War Sir Thomas Devitt and Sir Alfred Yarrow bought a 5,000-acre estate near Wokingham in Berkshire and the school moved there in 1921. Although it did not specifically train boys for the sea, for a long while many of them did take the sea option when they reached school-leaving age. The education and training they received was considered first class and not a few of the ex-pupils went on to gain high positions in the Mercantile Marine. In 1961 the number of orphans being cared for by the school had greatly reduced and, at the same time, the demand for sailors had drastically dropped. The school began to accept fee-payers, changed its name to Bearwood College and now runs as a public school.

Land-based nautical training became the norm as the 1920s and '30s wound on and many of the schools transferred from the old wooden walls to stone buildings ashore. However, those establishments that were conceived, designed and operated solely and purely as land-based schools offer a distinctly different view on training. Places like the Watts School were, in many ways, the forerunners of Royal Navy establishments such as HMS *Ganges* and the officer colleges at Dartmouth and Osborne. It is a fair legacy.

CHAPTER EIGHT
Schools Afloat – and a Few Ashore

For the last few years of the eighteenth and for virtually the whole of the nineteenth centuries there was a huge growth in the British Merchant Marine. Such a growth was linked to the Industrial Revolution, the enormous outpouring of manufacturing activity that turned Britain into the first truly industrial nation in the world. Within the space of a generation new businesses sprang up in virtually every part of the country and almost all of them soon began looking for new markets overseas. There was only one way to transport goods but the Merchant Navy was overstretched - it needed more ships and, of course, more men to sail them.

There had been a considerable amount of training available for seamen, particularly in the days of sail. Reformatory, industrial and charity ships had all played their part. However, by the second half of the nineteenth century little had been done towards keeping up the supply of officers trained in working sailing ships. Even as the shipping companies began to gradually adjust and turn over to steam powered vessels, there remained a preference – even a prejudice – for captains and officers who had learned their trade on sailing ships: 'It was regarded as a sterner and better school of navigation, in which was to be found a finer sort of seamanship; in which existed a stricter discipline. Such at any rate was the belief of many ship owners.'[84]

In an attempt to exploit this feeling, the Brassey Cadet Training Scheme was begun in 1890 and was the brainchild of Lord Brassey and Thomas Devitt. The idea was simple: they would provide proper training for apprentices on board working sailing ships. Parents would be asked to pay a larger premium to ensure that their sons learned about navigation and seafaring rather than simply how to polish brassware, which is what they received on most ships as apprentices.

It had become something of a custom for apprentices to be used as drudges, replacing the traditional cabin boys in carrying out all the dirty, unpleasant tasks on board ship. Few captains gave instruction in navigation and, as a result, fewer and fewer parents were inclined to send their sons to sea. A crisis was coming. Clearly something was needed to add to the good work being carried out by the *Conway* and *Worcester*, to help those boys who took the full sea option rather than the training ship route. The Brassey Scheme was born, then, on normal

The *Illawara* rounding Cape Horn decks awash. Trainees would endure conditions like this for days, even weeks, on end.

trading ships but trading ships that were fitted out for apprentices and with captains and crew who were genuinely interested in helping the newcomers.

Under the auspices of the Brassey Scheme, Devitt & Moore bought the *Hesperus* in 1890 and she began her first voyage, complete with a small group of apprentice cadets, a year later, arriving in Sydney after just eighty-eight days. There was a gold strike in Australia at this time and when the *Hesperus* docked the crew promptly quit the ship to seek their fortunes, leaving only the apprentices to manage the vessel during the four months she was waiting for a cargo. The ship undertook several other voyages, carrying her cargo and her cadets, her best run coming in 1892 when she made the trip to Melbourne in just seventy-one days.

The *Hesperus* apprentices were nothing if not full of fun. Once, when the ship was docked at Southampton, they left for a night ashore. The following day the pair of monumental lions on each side of the arch in the town's main street was found to have been given a coat of gold paint picked out with red spots courtesy of the boys. On another occasion they made puppets to resemble a number of pot plants and the pet cat of a short-sighted passenger and fooled her into thinking that they were dancing in the rain. It is to the credit of Capt Barrett, commander of the *Hesperus*, that none of these high-spirited pranks ever got a cadet 'logged'. Instead, he would simply invite the ringleader to dine with him, an occasion that invariably saw the boy emerge rather chastened and apologetic.

In 1899, the *Hesperus* was replaced by the *Illawara*, a 296-feet-long vessel built for comfort, not speed. She carried cadets and continued trading on the Australian route until 1907. Then she was sold off to a Norwegian company and was lost in the North Atlantic in 1912.

The *Harbinger* was also bought in 1890. A very fast ship, she measured 210 ft in length and carried cadets until 1897 when she was sold to the Russians for

Above left: The elegant *Macquarie*, all sails set.

Above right: Thomas Devitt, a hugely influential figure in the Brassey Cadet Scheme and the whole training process.

The *Port Jackson*, the ship that took one hundred Marine Society boys to Australia in 1907.

Left: The *Mersey,*owned and run by the White Star Line as a training ship for the Company.

Below: The *Pamir* and *Passat* are shown here in the docks at Penarth prior to their conversion into training ships.

£4,800. The *Macquarie* was the most famous of all Devitt & Moore's training ships. Built in 1875, she was a Blackwall frigate, originally called the *Melbourne*, and worked as a sea-borne training ship until 1904.

Accommodation for cadets on the *Macquarie* was taken out of the 'tween decks and a former dining saloon was also converted into a schoolroom. In all, the *Macquarie* undertook six voyages as a cadet ship between 1887 and 1903.

The scheme was meant to be self-funding. Premiums, or charges for parents, were set at £70 for the first voyage, £65 for the second and £60 for the third. Boys from the *Conway* and *Worcester*, however, received a reduced rate of £60 for the first two voyages and £50 for their third. The premium was payable at the beginning of each voyage and either party, parents or Devitt & Moore, was able to withdraw at the end. A number of boys did withdraw after their first trip, finding that the life did not suit them. Going aloft at night in dirty weather; seasickness; home-sickness; and, of course, the discipline that was essential on board ship; all these and more combined to separate the wheat from the chaff. However, if a boy did stick it then a long and successful career at sea was virtually guaranteed.[85]

In 1907, Devitt & Moore were contracted to take one hundred boys from the Marine Society ship, *Warspite*, for a round voyage to Australia. The idea was to train them at sea as deck-hands, but as Thomas Devitt had recently sold off the *Macquarie* the company had no suitable ship. Not daunted, Devitt promptly bought the *Port Jackson*, an iron-hulled sailing ship then lying in the Thames, waiting for a buyer.

It was an adventurous trip. Firstly, the captain of the *Port Jackson* died just three weeks before they set sail, then the ship damaged a number of her plates against the dockside, delaying by some days the start to the voyage. Then she was rammed, in a fog, by the German steamer, *Pyrgos*, while lying at anchor in the Downs. An 8 ft gash was carved into her side, cutting her to the water-line. The *Port Jackson* heeled over under the force of the impact and for a while it was thought the sailing vessel was doomed. As was reported in the press, the Marine Society boys all behaved admirably in the crisis: 'Chief Instructor Glynn at once ordered the bugler to blow the 'still', at which every boy stood to attention, silently awaiting whatever was to be.'[86]

Repairs delayed the *Port Jackson* by another month but when she finally left England she made good time and reached Sydney after 126 days. Interestingly, within six weeks of her return home all the Marine Society boys had managed to find berths in either the Merchant or Royal Navy. It had been an expensive experiment, however, and the Marine Society was obliged to reduce the number of boys to just fifty for the next voyage. The ship sailed on a number of further trips with Marine Society boys until the outbreak of war in 1914 put a stop to the scheme.

The year 1909 saw the formation of Devitt & Moore's Ocean Training Ships Ltd, a continuation of the Brassey Scheme. Shareholders included the Shaw Savill & Albion Line, Cunard and the Union Castle Line, shipping companies that clearly saw the advantages of such an idea. The *Port Jackson* was joined by the *Medway* in 1910 and, in the years leading up to the First World War, dozens of apprentice officers and deck-hands had their first taste of the sea on board one or the other of the Devitt & Moore ships. The scheme did not outlive the First World

Left: The beautiful and elegant stern section of the old paddler *Triton*.

Below: Moored at Sharpness near Gloucester, the *Vindicatrix* was the main base for the National Sea Training School. This view clearly shows the shore establishment that was built alongside the ship in 1945.

War, however, the *Port Jackson* being sold off at the end of 1916 in order to fund Devitt's new college at Pangbourne, while the *Medway* was requisitioned by the Admiralty in the final year of conflict.

There were one or two other ocean-going training ships operating out of British ports in the years before 1914. The Shaw Savill Line ran the *Euterpe* for twenty years until 1899, but the most famous of these ships was probably the White Star Line's *Mersey*. Launched in 1894, she was an iron sailing ship originally built for the Nourse Line who used her to transfer indentured Indian labourers to the Colonies.

In May 1908, the *Mersey* was bought by the White Star Line for use as a training ship. Running out of Liverpool, her aim was to train deck officers for the company. In 1914, she became the first sailing ship in the world to be equipped with radio and a year later achieved fame – or notoriety – when a successful operation for appendicitis was carried out on an apprentice during a cruise. Like many of these ships it was the First World War that spelled the end of her career, the White Star Line selling her for scrapping in 1915.

The British India Steam Navigation Company ran an apprentice training scheme until 1971 – using steam rather than sailing ships. The company had begun to recruit apprentices as early as 1906 but it was a further ten years before a formal cadet training scheme was introduced, although quite why the company should even consider this exercise in the middle of a major, worldwide conflict is a little confusing. It resulted in tragic consequences when the *Berbera*, en route from Bombay to Marseille, was torpedoed on 25 March 1917 with the loss of three cadets.

British India immediately commissioned two more trading and training ships, the *Waipara* and the *Carpentaria*. The *Waipara* was lost, torpedoed in August 1918, one cadet drowning in the disaster. Between 1916 and 1971 British India designated thirteen different ships as cadet training vessels, although, learning from their previous disasters, they suspended the programme during the Second World War. Boys who were engaged as apprentices or cadets acted as deck crew on the company ships but they were, at the same time, also given a structured programme of training.

The *Joseph Conrad* was part of an interesting experiment that took place in the 1930s. Launched in 1882 as the *Georg Stage*, she was originally used to train Dutch sailors but was bought in 1934 by Alan Villiers and renamed *Joseph Conrad* in honour of the great novelist, himself a sailor of some repute. Villiers' plan was to sail the ship around the world, crewed not by experienced sailors but by a party of boys. They left Ipswich on 22 October 1934 and sailed via New York, Rio de Janeiro, Cape Town and New Zealand, around Cape Horn, reaching New York again on 16 October 1938. In all, the ship and the boys travelled 57,000 miles. The *Joseph Conrad* is now moored in Mystic Seaport in Connecticut and is still used as a static training ship.

In the years after the Second World War many sailing ships were equipped and run as outward bound vessels, sometimes taking boys who wished to go to sea, at other times simply giving them an experience they would remember all their lives. The Aberdovey Outward Bound School, for example, ran such a ship, the *Garibaldi*, for several years.

The RNVR ship *Buzzard* was, for many years, a familiar sight to residents and visitors to London, lying just off Victoria Embankment.

The *Pamir Passat* Foundation was founded in the early 1950s, to train apprentice cadets on board two fully-rigged sailing ships, the *Pamir* and *Passat*. The vessels were intended for scrapping after the Second World War but were bought by a West German ship owner who intended to run them commercially. The enterprise proved uneconomical and the ships were acquired by the foundation. Moored in Penarth Dock, South Wales, they were duly converted into training and trading ships. Tragedy, however, was soon to follow.

In August 1957, the *Pamir* was lost in a hurricane in the Atlantic, over eighty officers, crew and young trainees losing their lives as the ship simply keeled over and disappeared into the depths of an unforgiving ocean. The *Passat* also ran into difficulties that year, her cargo shifting in heavy weather and the ship having to be towed into Lisbon with a severe list to port. The training of cadets on sea-going training sailing ships was promptly suspended and, apart from outward-bound vessels, has never really made a comeback.[87]

The Merchant Navy was not just concerned about recruiting officers. It also needed deck-hands, cooks, stokers, and all manner of sailors to run the ships that were so vital to Britain's survival. Consequently, Gravesend Sea School was established in 1918, just prior to the end of the First World War, an establishment that was intended to help re-man the Merchant Navy, replacing sailors who had been killed in the war. The school was located in what had once been the Commercial Hotel in Gravesend and had, since 1886, been used as a seamen's home.

The plan was to offer short but intensive training for boys aged between sixteen and seventeen who wished to become ratings in the Mercantile Marine. The first

The *President*, which succeeded the *Buzzard*.

admission arrived on Thursday 19 September 1918 and the school quickly grew to take 150 boys in all.

The old Royal Navy paddle ship, *Triton*, a beautiful little vessel with an elegant cruiser stern, was moored off Gravesend and this was where boys would undergo sea training and experience life afloat. The *Triton* had been launched in March 1882 as a Royal Navy survey ship. She was a composite vessel – iron-framed with wooden planking, the wood being sheathed in copper, presumably as protection against marine borers in the tropical seas where she was originally intended to work. Between 1902 and 1919, she operated as a Royal Navy training ship before becoming part of the Gravesend Sea School, a role she carried out until 1930 when she was sold to the Ministry of Transport, taken to West India Dock and became part of the National Sea Training Schools. Managed by the Shipping Federation, she was the base where men were taught and tested in boat handling in order to gain their AB rating.

In 1926, the old sailing ship, *Vindicatrix*, also became involved with Gravesend Sea School when she was towed to a mooring off the town. She was to be used as an accommodation hulk for boys and staff of the school while alterations were carried out on the buildings. The *Vindicatrix* had led a chequered life, being launched as the *Arranmoor* before being bought by a German company, renamed *Waltraute* and used as a parent ship for German U-boats during the First World War. After the war she returned to working under the Red Ensign! Lying off Gravesend, the *Vindicatrix*, now renamed for the third time, was rammed by a Swedish steamer but the damage was slight and in July, with building work at the school completed, she was taken to West India Dock where she became the first seamanship school for the Shipping Federation, soon to be joined by the *Triton*.

The *Eaglet* was a Royal Naval Reserve training ship moored at Liverpool.

In 1939, with war hovering on the horizon, it was felt that the boys of Gravesend Sea School would be safer away from London: 'The site chosen would need to have access to open water for boat-training purposes and accommodation for several hundred boys and staff, but at the same time be away from what might be considered essential targets by the enemy.'[88]

Before too long the site was fixed, a small backwater off the canal at Sharpness in Gloucestershire, and accommodation, it was decided, would be provided once more on the old *Vindicatrix*. The old ship was duly taken from West India Dock and moored at Gravesend until, on 8 June 1939, she was towed out towards the open sea. The journey down the Channel, around the tip of Cornwall and up the Bristol Channel took four days. The *Vindicatrix* arriving in Sharpness Dock at 1810 hr on Monday 12 June.

Over the next few years training went on with increased urgency as more and more ships and men were lost at sea. The *Vindicatrix* certainly had a wartime look about her, sandbags being used to protect the upper deck and a pair of Lewis guns mounted to guard against air attack. Conditions on board were very cramped. A camp alongside the ship was planned but wartime restrictions on use of building materials meant that this was not completed until 1945. When it was finished the camp, built on land known as the Plantation, consisted of twenty wooden and asbestos huts. Once it was completed numbers at the school rose rapidly, 500 boys being trained at any one time. The *Vindicatrix* was used to sleep up to sixty boys in turn on the boat deck, giving them the valuable experience of sleeping on board ship, probably for the first time in their whole lives.

Conditions in these war and immediately post-war years were not easy and discipline was rigidly enforced. There was a job to do and the instructors knew that what they were teaching could, as like as not, save a boy's life: 'Boys came

Another RNR vessel, the *Daedlaus*, served at Bristol for many years before being finally broken up in 1911.

from every walk of life and many at the age of 16 were what today we would call 'streetwise' and their backgrounds were such that they could easily cope with their spell at the "Vindi"; others could not. As it was, most weeks someone "went over the fence" and tried to make it home and others, in their private desperation, signed on foreign ships in Sharpness Docks.'[89]

Courses were originally fourteen weeks in duration for deck boys and ten for stewards. Later this was changed to twelve and eight respectively. The curriculum was basic but vitally important if the trainees were to survive at sea. Here, amongst other things, boys learned how to launch a lifeboat, box a compass or prepare food and serve it in tiny galleys hardly suited for the purpose.

After the war ended the Gravesend Sea Training School returned to the Thames but the *Vindicatrix* had proved so useful an establishment that it was decided to retain her at Sharpness. Despite being part of what was now known as the National Sea Training Schools, the boys in training and the officers who instructed them on the ship no longer considered themselves anything to do with Gravesend – indeed, in the immediate post-war period both establishments took very parochial stances, each viewing the other as the 'opposition.'

With the old *Vindicatrix* looking more ancient by the day, plans to build modern classrooms alongside the Sharpness canal fell through in the early 1960s. At the same time planning permission was granted for a new school at Gravesend and work commenced in late 1963. It effectively spelled the end for the *Vindicatrix*. The National Sea Training School was renamed the National Sea Training College and moved to its new premises on Chalk Marshes in 1967. That January, watched by thousands of local people who had grown up with the image of the ship always in their minds eye, three tugs towed the old *Vindicatrix* from her berth at Sharpness to Newport on the River Usk where she was broken up. She had served for twenty-seven years as a training ship, some 70,000 boys passing up her gangplank.

The college at Gravesend continued to flourish for several more years although the original buildings were demolished in 1975. In 2003, however, due to the continued decline in the size of the Merchant Marine and, as a consequence, a reduction in student numbers, the college closed. The premises on Chalk Marshes became a Metropolitan Police College.

There were many more school ships based around the coast of Britain during the nineteenth and twentieth centuries but, mostly, these were intended for training men, not boys. Probably the most famous were the Royal Naval Volunteer Reserve ships that lay, for many years, off the Victoria Embankment in London. These were the *Rainbow*, which was succeeded by the *Frolic*, and, in particular, the *Buzzard* and the *President*. The RNVR was a civilian force for the Royal Navy, occupying a position roughly similar to that of the Territorial Army, each entrant being trained and prepared to serve with the regular forces as and when required.

The Royal Naval Reserve, established in 1861, originally consisted of ratings only, officers not being appointed until some time later. However, when they were appointed many boys from training ships like the *Conway* and *Worcester*, although serving in the Merchant Navy, became RNR officers.

The RNR maintained a number of training ships around the coast, using them as training bases and drill ships for sailors. The *Eaglet* began life as HMS *Eagle*, a third-rate, seventy-four-gun battleship that was launched in 1804. When she was paid-off at Devonport in 1848 she was laid up for a while before becoming a coastguard ship at Milford Haven. Due for breaking up, in 1862 she was reprieved and taken to Liverpool to act as a drill ship for the RNR. During the First World War she flew the flag of Rear Admiral Stileman and when the new aircraft carrier, *Eagle*, was commissioned her name was changed to *Eaglet*. Sold for breaking in 1926 she was beached at Mostyn and in April 1927 was accidentally burnt out as she lay.

The *Daedlaus*, a twenty-gun corvette, was launched at Sharpness and served until 1861. Thereafter she went to Bristol as an RNR vessel. Moored for many years at Mardyke Ferry she was finally broken up in 1911. There were many more vessels like the *Eaglet* and *Daedlaus* but as they were intended primarily for seamen, they lie outside the general outlines of this book.

Sea-going merchant ships, even land-based establishments like Gravesend and stationary training vessels like the *President*, *Buzzard* and *Daedlaus* are now a thing of the past. Yet in their heyday they were an important part of British life. People saw them or read and heard about them, training boys to continue answering the 'essential calling of the sea'. They were undoubtedly proud to see the old vessels moored to the riverbanks or battling up the Channel. They made them feel safe; they made them feel British.

CHAPTER NINE
The Senior Service – Royal Naval Schools for Boys

During the first half of the nineteenth century, training for boy sailors in the Royal Navy was almost non-existent. What limited training there was available was chaotic, badly organised and without much sense of purpose. It was the middle decade of the century before the government at last made a serious attempt to look at the problems of how to supply the Navy with sailors, without having to resort to the infamous press-gang.

The 1859 Report on Manning the Navy was clear on the point that boys received into the Royal Navy at an early age became more attached to the service and far better sailors than men who joined later: 'so sensible are we to the advantages of early training that we recommend that a large ship . . . capable of affording accommodation to 500 boys, should be placed at Plymouth; and that four additional training vessels should be provided, which would enable the whole of the boys required for the Navy to receive the same instruction. This would entail an expense of about £15,918 per annum.'[90]

It was not as if there was no training available. The *Excellent* had been in existence as a training ship, more particularly as a gunnery ship, for twenty years but she dealt primarily with men, not boys, and by 1859 barely 3,000 sailors had passed across her decks. A number of training brigs had been in commission for some time, cruising in home waters and invariably carrying out some discreet and low-key recruiting. In general, however, during the first half of the century most boys who entered the Navy simply signed on and received whatever training their captains thought appropriate as the ship went about its normal duties. However, things were changing.

After July 1853 all new boy entrants were engaged for periods of ten years service and the opportunity for promotion from boy to ordinary seaman was greatly improved. Pensions were now payable after twenty years (after the age of eighteen) and standards on entry greatly tightened up. Pay was increased and paid leave between commissions was also introduced. Punishment, so long a brutal and dangerous practice that had been down to the vagaries of individual captains, became more regulated, officers being urged to be more moderate in their language and in the use of corporal punishment.

Cutlass drill on a Royal Navy training ship.

Training ships specifically for boy entrants into the Navy were at last created when, in 1854, the old two-decker, *Illustrious*, was established at Portsmouth. A year later she was followed by the *Implacable* at Devonport. Capt Robert Harris immediately designed and introduced a one-year course of seamanship instruction on the *Illustrious*, a highly effective and enlightened system that was recorded by a boy sailor calling himself simply 'John' and published in book form in 1862 as *A Sailor Boy's Logbook*.

In his book John describes the training programme in some detail. After getting out to the *Illustrious*, which lay half a mile off shore and informing the petty officer on board that he wanted to enlist, he was given a handful of biscuits and told to bed himself down for the night. He was given a mattress and blanket and these he promptly spread out on the orlop deck and, using some nearby round shot as a pillow, soon dropped off to sleep. He was woken next morning to shouts of 'Show a leg!' and given half a pint of cocoa for breakfast. After a medical examination he duly signed on for his ten-year stint as a sailor. Then his training began in earnest.

First instruction, as he called it, was a three-day course of learning to tie elementary knots and how to lash a hammock. Second instruction consisted of boat pulling, learning to row, scull and launch the longboats, while third instruction took the form of cutlass and rifle drill. Apparently the new recruits fired at old stakes in the mud at low tide.

Fourth instruction was how to use the ship's cannons, including how to train and dismount the massive guns. Fifth instruction was mastering more complicated rope work before the trainees moved on to the sixth instruction, which consisted of working on a model sailing ship, fully rigged, in the schoolroom. Seventh,

Right: Going up the rigging and over the futtock shrouds – an essential component in the training of all boy sailors.

Below: The *Impregnable*, almost an exact replica of the *Victory*, old but still impressive even after her sea-going days were over.

The first *Boscawen*, a 70-gun warship brought to Portland as a training ship in 1866.

and last, instruction was in handling a lead-line and learning the points of the compass. After that, as John says, they were passed out as boy sailors.

The whole process had taken six months – care and compassion being used to inform, educate and instruct rather than the brutality that had so often been commonplace in the past – and the boys were then sent to the training brig *Sealark* for a number of short cruises in the Channel. After three months on the *Sealark* it was back to the *Illustrious* for another three months when he and his companions could improve themselves in any aspect they chose of their new profession.[91] It was light-years ahead of what boys in Nelson's Navy could expect but it was the future, the way that all naval training was now going.

During the second half of the nineteenth century training for boy seamen in the Royal Navy finally began to be taken seriously. The *Lion* joined *Implacable* at Devonport in 1871, being moored bow to stern with the older vessel in Hamoze Creek off Torpoint. Fifteen years later, a third ship, the *Impregnable*, almost an exact copy of Nelson's *Victory*, was added to the pair, thus creating the largest pre-sea training establishment for boys in the whole Navy. The three ships were, together, known as HMS *Impregnable*. The establishment was further increased by the arrival of HMS *Circe* in 1874. She operated under her own name until 1916 when she was rechristened *Impregnable IV*.

The seventy-gun *Boscawen* was brought to Portland in October 1866 but she soon proved too small to offer effective training for boy sailors. As a result the larger *Trafalgar*, which was quickly renamed *Boscawen*, replaced her and a shore training complex was built on Portland Bill, above the dockyard, in 1882. The *Minotaur* and *Agincourt*, both ironclad warships, joined the establishment in 1893 and 1904 respectively, becoming *Boscawen II* and *Boscawen III*.

Excellent and *Calcutta* at Portsmouth, the Navy gunnery school – at the bottom right, just visible ahead of *Calcutta*, are the *Vernon* and *Ariadne*, torpedo school for the Navy.

HMS *St Vincent*, a 120-gun ship of the line, began training boy sailors in Portsmouth Harbour in 1862. Here she joined HMS *Excellent* which, although primarily a gunnery school, was also used as a boys' training ship. As late as 1869 a mizzen-mast was kept rigged on board in order to offer sail training to the boys. When the mud-flats around the ship were exposed by the low tide, *Excellent* flew a red flag to show that firing was about to take place – the shot was recovered by 'mudlarks' who then promptly sold them back to the ship. The 'mudlarks' apparently had wooden boards strapped to their feet and on these they would ski across the glutinous mud. On a good day these enterprising characters could expect to earn as much as eleven shillings a head.[92]

For a short while the *St Vincent* and *Excellent* kept company with the old *Illustrious*, the original boys' training ship. By now, however, the *Illustrious* was getting old and in 1868, just a few years after the *St Vincent* was established, she was towed away for breaking.

Despite the fact that Portsmouth and Plymouth had long been the heartland of the Royal Navy, the training of boy sailors was not just restricted to the south coast of England. Ireland and Scotland could also boast Royal Navy training ships, usually – but not exclusively – taking entrants from those areas.

The 9,210-ton ironclad *Black Prince* was established as a training ship at Queenstown in Southern Ireland in 1896. She operated under that name until a modern cruiser, also called *Black Prince*, was launched in March 1904, whereupon the Irish training ship had to be rechristened and was given the new name of *Emerald*. Her time as a training ship was short-lived, however, the establishment

The *Caledonia* was moored for a few years at Queensferry on the Firth of Forth, taking Scottish boys for training.

closing in 1910, just fourteen years after it was established. The training ship herself was not scrapped but moved back to Plymouth where she joined the *Impregnable* establishment. She survived in this role until February 1923 when she was finally sold off for breaking up.

The *Caledonia* was opened at Queensferry on the Firth of Forth in 1891. The ship was actually the old *Impregnable* which had been stationed at Devonport until 1886 when she had been replaced as the boys' training ship by the Pembroke Dock-built *Howe*, renamed 'Impregnable,' as tradition demanded. The old *Impregnable* was rechristened *Caledonia*, refitted at Devonport and given more modern armament, specifically for training purposes. Then, on 10 October 1891, she was towed north by the cruiser, *Aurora*, to her new base near Queensferry.

Moored at Port Edgar, Leith, the *Caledonia* had a complement of 171 officers, instructors and boy trainees. On 3 November 1892, she was joined by the *Wanderer*; this small ship being designated as a tender and as a vessel that could give the boys experience of life afloat.

As early as 1894 there were concerns about the location of the *Caledonia*. On 12 January a question in the House of Commons made members aware that a number of trainees on the ship had recently become unwell. It was not the first incidence of illness on board the ship. Mr S. Smith, the member for Flint, posed the question: 'I beg to ask the Secretary for Scotland whether he is aware that very many of the boys in the training ship 'Caledonia' have been ill with pneumonia; and that it is considered the ship is very unhealthy, from the long continuance of infectious disease; and whether the Government will consider the advisability of removing the boys to another ship?'[93]

HMS *Ganges*, seen here off Harwich shortly before the famous shore establishment was opened.

The response came from Sir U. Kay-Shuttleworth. Yes, there had been instances of pneumonia on the ship but not more than might be reasonably expected in Scotland at that time of year. The general health of the boys on board was considered good and there were no grounds to suppose the ship unhealthy. Therefore the Admiralty saw no reason whatsoever to move the trainees to another ship.[94]

Perhaps the most famous naval establishment for the training of boy sailors was HMS *Ganges*, first opened as a training ship in 1865. She was a teak-built, eighty-four-gun vessel with a displacement of 3,600 tons and, to begin with, was based in Falmouth Harbour. She remained at Falmouth until 1899 when, as part of the reorganisation of naval training then taking place, she set sail for a new base at Harwich. She was anchored off the port with a view of Shotley peninsula across the bay.

In 1906, the transition was made from ship to shore-based training when the earliest buildings – and the infamous *Ganges'* mast – were erected at Shotley Gate. This new training school was to be known as RN Training Establishment, Shotley. Soon, more huts, playing fields, a school, gymnasium and a swimming pool were added to the establishment. The old hulk remained, moored to the pier, until 1929 when she was towed away for breaking and the original name was then reinstated.

From the beginning *Ganges* was notorious for the ferocity of its regime. Lashings and whippings with three-foot-long bamboo canes, lengths of wire threaded through the hollow middle of the canes, were commonplace. To the regret of many instructors, soon after the shore establishment was created, some diminution of punishments was brought in: 'Maximum punishment was reluctantly lowered from

Left: The infamous *Ganges* mast, festooned with boy sailors.

Below: Physical fitness was always important at *Ganges* and this posed view shows young trainees and their instructors in the gymnasium at Shotley.

The liner *Majestic* (the ex-German *Bismarck*), renamed *Caledonia*, took up a mooring at Rosyth in 1937 – her life as a training ship was short.

thirty-two lashes to twelve, a rule that remained until the final lowering of the White Ensign in October 1976.'[95]

Punishment did not just come in the shape of a cane, however. Running up and down Laundry Hill or Faith, Hope and Charity – three flights of stone steps that led to the weed-encrusted foreshore – were also commonly used ways of dealing with miscreants and were favourite sanctions of what were called 'hard-hearted, soft-headed' instructors. Naval police, the dreaded 'Crushers', led by the 'jaunty' (the master-at-arms), controlled the campus with a rod of iron.

The school had ten divisions, all named after famous admirals – Exmouth Division, Benbow Division, and so on – with five messes to each one. The five messes comprised three seamen's messes, one communications mess and a 'floater' that carried the overspill from the others. One tradition of the school, the first that anyone encountered, was that every boy had to climb the mast before leaving the 'annexe' (the nursery where new recruits, known as 'nozzers', were first placed in order to be sorted into the right division and mess). HMS *Ganges*, proper, lay like a bad dream just across the way!

On special days – a visiting admiral or Parents' Day or, perhaps, the sovereign's birthday – the mast would be full of boys, all standing equidistant on the rigging and the yardarms with the button boy on the very top. This was a special honour, each incumbent always being presented with a button boy's medal. Privileges were granted – but rarely: 'Privileges was the name the Navy gave to anything that any normal human being could expect from life – like living. Eating was a privilege . . . . Another privilege was freedom. Freedom was the name given to a period of time when they ran out of ideas to keep a boy busy.'[96]

Boys on the deck of a training ship learning how to tie knots and splices.

At the end of the nineteenth and beginning of the twentieth centuries the Navy began to rationalise its training facilities for boys. The newly planned barracks at Shotley meant that many of the old wooden walls were now obsolete. As a result the *St Vincent* was sold for scrap in 1906, although twenty years later the establishment reopened in the old Royal Marine barracks in Gosport and continued to provide training until 1968. *Caledonia* and *Boscawen* both closed for good in 1906. The pattern was unpredictable, however. The *Lion* was sold off in 1905, the *Implacable* in 1908, but while plans had been laid to get rid of the *Impregnable*, a sudden flood of boys into the Royal Navy meant that the Admiralty had to adjust its thinking. As a result, *Impregnable* was retained and HMS *Inconstant* added to the training school – to be joined by *Emerald* a few years later.

It did not take a great deal of insight to see, as early as 1910, that war with Germany was inevitable at some stage in the not too distant future. And, as a result, a new training establishment was set up at Devonport. Based around HMS *Powerful* this opened in 1913. The *Powerful* was renamed *Impregnable* and continued to work until the last draft of boys left in January 1929 and the establishment moved ashore to a set of barracks at Bull Point.

The name *Caledonia* was given a new lease of life in Scotland when another training ship of that name was created on the Firth of Forth in 1937. She was a 56,551-ton liner, originally called *Bismarck*, and launched in Germany in 1914. At the time of her launch she was the largest ship in the world, a record she held until superseded by the *Normandie* in 1935. Taken over and given to the White Star Line in 1919 as compensation for war losses, she was renamed *Majestic* and operated as their flagship for several years.

HMS *Britannia* – with the *Hindustan* moored just ahead – in the river at Dartmouth.

By the mid-1930s the *Majestic* was laid up at Southampton and in May 1935 was actually sold to the firm of T. W. Ward for scrapping. Then it was discovered that, by the terms under which she was handed to the White Star Line, she could not be sold. So Ward's received twenty-four obsolete destroyers instead, the equivalent in scrap value of the liner, and *Majestic* was converted into a training ship. Equipped to take 1,500 young naval cadets, the ship was renamed *Caledonia* and taken to Rosyth where she began her training role on 23 April 1937.

When war broke out in September 1939 the Admiralty felt that the *Caledonia* would be too tempting a target for enemy bombers and submarines and, as a consequence, all her cadets came ashore. The ship was anchored out in the Forth until the Admiralty decided what to do with her. When fire broke out on the ship later that month the Admiralty's decision was made for them and *Caledonia*'s brief career as a training ship was over, almost before it had begun.

By the beginning of the twentieth century about a quarter of the entry intake for the Royal Navy came from the boys' training schools. Boys were accepted between the ages of fifteen and sixteen and a half. The qualifications required were signed permission from the parents, the ability to read and write, a clean record and a character reference from a person of some significance. There was also an academic test and certain physical standards had to be met. Basic training usually took between nine and fifteen months, after which time boys were rated as boy seaman first class. At the age of eighteen they became ordinary seamen.

During the 1920s and 30s many vessels were used to give boys experience of life at sea, cruisers like the *Cumberland* and battleships such as the *Benbow* and *Empress of India* all carrying out the role for short periods. In February 1937 the boys' gunnery school, HMS *Pembroke* was opened on the Medway. It led a

Cadets working in the Chart Study on *Britannia*.

rather chequered life, however, closing, opening and having various uses until final closure came in October 1959.

Separate sea training for boys in the Royal Navy ended after the closure of *St Vincent* in 1968 and *Ganges* in 1973. Although boys still enter the Navy directly on leaving school, their training is now delivered parallel with adult new entries. The Navy had always used ships to train men sailors, establishments like *Excellent*, *Vernon and Ariadne*, *Fisguard* and *Defiance*. These usually had a specific aim or purpose. *Excellent*, for example, was a gunnery school; *Defiance* an electrical and torpedo school. When, inevitably, these establishments came ashore, they brought their names with them so that the gunnery school at Whale Island was always known as HMS *Excellent*.

Officer training, like that for ratings, was poorly organised during the first half of the nineteenth century. Although the Royal Naval Academy had been founded at Portsmouth in 1733 it was never a popular route to a commission. Patronage and family connections – plus a belief that nothing could ever make up for practical experience learned on the quarterdeck – meant that, for many years, there was considerable prejudice against the graduates of the academy. Most potential officers simply joined a ship and learned from the old hands or from instructors on board ship.

Nevertheless, the academy remained popular with those who attended the establishment and for youngsters without connections or means it did provide an important first step on the ladder. There was an incentive. For graduates of the academy there was a 'fast-track' to becoming a lieutenant, the period being shortened from six to just four years. Interestingly, two of Jane Austen's brothers, Francis and Charles, both attended the academy, the Austen family being decidedly short on influence and connections, and both rose to the rank of admiral.

Despite the growing influence of steam and oil, instruction in sailing and seamanship were still essential elements of a young officer's trade.

There was some reorganisation and a short gap in provision after 1806 when the Admiralty revised the curriculum and replaced the academy with a new Royal Navy college, operating, like its predecessor, out of the dockyard at Portsmouth. This opened in 1808 and ran until it closed as an officer-training establishment in 1837. Thereafter it continued as a training college for senior officers. Part of the problem was that opposition to the academy and the college had continued, some captains being so prejudiced that they even refused to accept college-trained cadets on board their ships. Clearly, some new way of training young officers was required.

The Admiralty introduced the rank of cadet in 1843, for all boys intending to become lieutenants. And from 1857 it was decided that all cadets would be instructed on board a training ship at anchor before proceeding to sea. At first this work began on board the *Illustrious*, where Capt Robert Harris was still in command, but from 1859 officer training was centred on the old, first-rate *Britannia*. To begin with, *Britannia* was moored in Haslar Creek in Portsmouth Harbour, one of the earliest cadets to join being Lord Charles Beresford who later rose to the highest pinnacle in the Navy and to command of the Channel Fleet. Beresford was promoted to cadet captain on board the *Britannia* but demoted the same day after celebrating by emptying the contents of a bread bin over the master-at-arms – and making the mistake of staying around to get caught!

Beresford was the man – or boy, as he then was – whose naval career almost stalled before it began. At his interview he was asked if he always spelled William, his middle name, with one l. Beresford considered for a moment, then shrugged and said, 'only sometimes.' He passed and was duly admitted to *Britannia*. Perhaps the story says as much about the academic standards of trainee officers as it does about Beresford's quickness of thought.

The Royal Naval College at Osborne on the Isle of Wight.

Portsmouth in those days had rather an unsavoury reputation – hardly the best of spots to train young officers. So the *Britannia* was sailed around the coast to Portland. It was not a good move, the exposed position making boat work difficult and restricting communications with the land. When cadets did manage to get ashore there was little in the way of sport or leisure, apart from cliff climbing, and when one boy was killed by a fall from the cliff it was clear that the *Britannia* would have to move again. This time her destination was a river estuary where access to and from shore was relatively easy.[97]

In 1863 the *Britannia* was moored in the River Dart, just off the small town of Dartmouth. Within a few terms there were over 300 cadets in training on board, the large number causing huge congestion on the sleeping decks and in the mess rooms. Capt Powell – who had relieved Capt Harris only the year before – complained to the Admiralty and in 1864 *Britannia* was joined by the *Hindustan*, an old two-decker built of Indian teak. She was moored ahead of *Britannia* and a walkway or covered gangway built between the two ships.

The year 1869 saw the old *Britannia* replaced by a newer and larger vessel, the name being retained, as ever. The training period was for two years and after passing out cadets were appointed to a sea-going training ship (first the *Bristol* and later the *Ariadne*) for a further year. In 1877 Prince Edward and Prince George, the sons of the Prince of Wales (later King Edward VII) were admitted to *Britannia*. They arrived at a time of some controversy.

Cadet J. E. Lloyd had just been dismissed from the ship and labelled as 'idle and troublesome . . . worthless and unfit to be an officer.' His father complained and, while he was clear that he did not want his son to return to the ship, he did demand an inquiry. Lloyd, it was alleged, had been bullied by other cadets, had also been forced to sing in the mess room and had his pocket money stolen. There

Under the influence of Jackie Fisher, all officers had to have knowledge of machinery, engineering and science. This view shows Osborne boys at work in their laboratory.

was not enough evidence to substantiate the charges but, as a result of the inquiry, in 1894, the new captain, A. W. Moore, introduced a more closely supervised system of control with lieutenants having particular charge of each term and maintaining a close watch on all cadets.[98]

Conditions on board were undoubtedly harsh, often deliberately so. First thing in the morning all cadets had to plunge into a cold, seawater bath on the upper deck while going 'over the masthead' was something that became compulsory for everyone. Falling from the futtocks was common, though nets above the deck and the rigging did cut down on serious injury. Punishments varied from isolation, restricted diet and wearing a distinctive white band to having to carry a weighted wooden bar and, of course, corporal punishment. Canings were carried out on the poop deck, the victim being bent over a 'horse' from the gymnasium. To the command 'Young Gentlemen, 'shun' everyone came to attention while the punishment – six strokes or twelve – was carried out by one of the chief petty officers.

There were compensations. On the nearby playing field a retired petty officer and his wife ran a canteen for the cadets where a 'garry sandwich' – a piece of cream chocolate squashed between two Garibaldi biscuits – was, for many years, the most popular item on the menu. Perhaps more interestingly, the old petty officer had a daughter who, for a penny a head – always provided there were not less than seven cadets in the party – would take the boys up to the woods where she would happily pull up her skirts and offer a different but equally vital piece of education.

By the end of the nineteenth century it was time for change once more and, on Christmas Day 1902, the Admiralty announced a long awaited new process of

Carpentry work at Osborne.

training for naval officers. The Selbourne Scheme – named after the First Lord of the Admiralty, the Earl of Selbourne – was actually the result of intense research and consultation by one of the most charismatic and important figures in naval history, the Second Sea Lord, Jackie Fisher.

Fisher's plan was to create a common entry and training programme for officers of the three main branches of the Navy – executive, engineer and Royal Marine. He was clear that all officers should be engineers as the modern Navy depended on machinery and, most importantly of all, that education and training should be completed before officers went to sea, and should not drag on throughout their early days of service.[99]

There was some opposition, many officers feeling that it was ungentlemanly to venture anywhere near the engine room of a ship, but Jackie Fisher was undaunted. He had already planned a new land-based college at Dartmouth to replace the old *Britannia* and *Hindustan* but he also wanted to create a junior college, a place that would educate younger boys before they were eligible for Dartmouth. The site he chose was the 2,000-acre Osborne estate on the Isle of Wight. It had been owned by Queen Victoria, was her favourite residence and was where she had died in 1901. Edward VII detested the place as it reminded him of his unhappy childhood and on his coronation day he presented the property to the nation. His original plan was for the property to be used as a convalescent home for Royal Navy officers, but Jackie Fisher had no trouble in persuading the King that part of the house and estate should be used for his new junior college.

Osborne was duly equipped with engineering workshops and classrooms and the cruiser, *Racer*, was provided to offer training afloat. Fees were set at £75 per annum and, after a stiff examination, candidates faced a panel of senior naval officers including, whenever possible, Jackie Fisher himself – a terrifying

The elegant Royal Naval College at Dartmouth, opened in 1905.

experience for any twelve year old boy to endure: 'many a good candidate was reduced to incoherence by the awfulness of the occasion – and failed. The lucky ones faced four years of Spartan training and membership of a unique band of brothers. Among them, over successive years, were four royal princes; the three brothers who became respectively Kings Edward VIII and George VI and the Duke of Kent, and their cousin Admiral of the Fleet Earl Mountbatten.'[100]

The first seventy cadets joined Osborne in September 1903. They remained there for two years before moving to the beautiful new college at Dartmouth, designed by Sir Aston Webb on the hill above the River Dart, to complete their final two years of training. The *Britannia*'s last entry of cadets left the ship in September 1905, being accommodated on two cruisers based on Bermuda. It was a temporary arrangement as from January 1906 it was intended that all naval cadets would go to Osborne and/or Dartmouth College for their training.

One establishment that became a victim of Fisher's reforms was the Royal Naval Engineering College, Keyham. Opened in 1880 specifically to train naval engineering officers, the college replaced the hulk, *Marlborough*, which had been operating for the previous ten years. Trainees spent five years at the college, then a further two at Greenwich before being posted to ships as assistant engineers.

With Jackie Fisher's insistence that all naval officers were now engineers, the college was something of an anachronism and closed in 1910. However, with war looming the establishment was reopened in April 1914 when it was used to train special entry cadets. It returned to training engineers in 1919 and in 1938, due to an urgent need to expand, moved to new premises at Manadon. The establishment was renamed *Thunderer* in 1947 and continued operating until 1994 when all engineer training for the Navy was passed over to Southampton University.

When war came in August 1914, the Royal Naval College at Dartmouth was cleared of its cadets, all 420 of them, including that summer's intake from Osborne. These young boys, some barely fifteen years old, were sent to man the ships of the Reserve Fleet, vessels that were in the process of being rapidly recommissioned.

Thirteen of these cadets went gladly and unknowingly to their deaths when the old cruisers *Aboukir*, *Hogue* and *Cressy* were torpedoed and sunk by a German submarine on 22 September. Countless more died during the four-year conflict, doing their duty as it had been explained and instilled in them at the Royal Naval Colleges of Dartmouth and Osborne.

At the end of the war it quickly became apparent that Britain did not require – and, indeed, could not afford - the huge Navy that had been built up in the years before 1914. Numbers of boys applying for places at Osborne began to drop rapidly away; clearly the place was no longer economically viable. As a result Osborne closed in May 1923. In future all naval-officer training for boy entrants would take place at Dartmouth.

The Royal Navy is now a streamlined and effective service but, in comparison to the gigantic fleets that were maintained in the nineteenth and early twentieth centuries, it is 'small fry.' Like the Navy itself, training establishments have been reduced and cut back. Yet the glorious days of the past are still there, even if only in the memories of historians and those who experienced them.

CHAPTER TEN

Fire, Wreck and a Bombing

Of all the potential dangers that menaced and threatened wooden warships, the most lethal was undoubtedly fire. If fire ever broke out on board a wooden wall the only chance was to catch it early, but in the dark, narrow confines of ancient hulls, where planks were sealed and coated in tar, where flammable materials lay across the decks like sleeping mountains, this was almost an impossible task. Seven training ships were destroyed by fire over the years, sometimes by accident, sometimes by deliberate action, and there were many other instances of arson attacks being foiled in the nick of time.

Interestingly, none of the Royal Navy training ships were destroyed in this way, at least while they were working. Such disasters seemed to be reserved solely for the reformatory, industrial and charity vessels. The only RN vessel to meet her end by fire was the *Caledonia*, the ex-German liner that had been commissioned by the Royal Navy in 1937, and by the time she was destroyed in the early days of the Second World War she had already been devoid of cadets for several weeks. Empty, forlorn and moored in the Firth of Forth while the Admiralty pondered on her fate, the *Caledonia* mysteriously caught fire and sank at her moorings on 29 September 1939. The hull was eventually raised on 17 July 1943 and used as scrap metal for the war effort.

For the wooden warships of the Victorian age, fire was an ever-present hazard. The industrial school ship from the Forest Gate Workhouse, the 190-foot *Goliath*, met her end off Grays on the Thames in December 1875. It was just three days before Christmas, a dark and dismal Wednesday morning, and the boys were clearing the decks after breakfast.

At ten minutes to eight, thirteen-year-old Robert Loeber, the trainee in charge of the lamps on the ship's main deck, was in the process of putting away the lights that were always kept burning all night. He had extinguished nine out of the twelve and was moving on to the next when he burned his hand on the loop that suspended it and dropped the light onto the lamp-room floor. The floor was soaked in oil and immediately erupted in flames. Loeber hurled his serge jumper onto the fire in a desperate attempt to smother the blaze but it was no use. At the later inquest it was suggested that he had panicked and thrown the contents of an

'No my boy, I must be last. That's the way at sea.' Lance Calkin's romanticised view of the destruction of the *Goliath* shows Captain Bourchier on his stricken ship – it was actually posed against the *Exmouth*, the replacement vessel for the *Goliath*.

The second *Warspite*, destroyed by fire in 1918.

The mess room of the industrial training ship *Wellesley*, burned to the waterline in 1914.

oilcan onto the fire, mistaking it for water – Loeber strenuously denied the charge and the matter was dropped.

One of the other boys soon spotted the flames and, with panic clawing at his throat, reported it to the chief officer. The fire bell was rung and Capt Bourchier alerted but it was already too late. Within three minutes the main deck was ablaze. All of the ship's ports were open and, with the wind blowing hard from the west, the flames were quickly fanned. Boys were well drilled and knew what to do. In unison they ran to their emergency stations but the fire hoses were burned through and, almost before they knew it, they were driven away from the pumps by the ferocity of the fire.

The *Goliath* lay about 1,000 yards off shore and, given the weather conditions and the severity of the fire, launching the lifeboats proved difficult. The flames destroyed several of them long before they could be lowered from the davits; others fell into the water and were smashed or simply drifted away when the ropes that held them were cut in a desperate effort to get them afloat. At the time there was a water barge alongside and, thanks to the efforts of trainee William Bolton, over a hundred boys were able to use this to get ashore. Thirteen-year-old Bolton was later awarded a silver medal by the Liverpool Royal Humane Society for his bravery and presented with a silver watch from the local government board.

Within ten minutes of seeing the smoke, the nearby *Arethusa* had sent several boats to help the stricken *Goliath*, along with other vessels from Grays and Gravesend. On board the *Goliath* there were several acts of heroism. The chief carpenter, Mr Thompson, discovered a group of boys trapped in a storeroom. He broke off the iron bars over the ports to allow them to escape and later escaped himself by diving into the river and baling out a floating boat with his boots. Dragging ten boys out of the river he then somehow managed to get the boat to shore.

This postcard view gives a good indication of the training received on many of the training ships.

Capt Bourchier stood on the gangway, urging the boys to leave the ship. At one point he threw some breadboxes into the river and insisted that boys use these as life rafts. His wife and two daughters, who lived on board with him, had already been rescued but only after Mrs Bourchier had made a jump of twenty-five feet into the Thames. Capt Bourchier stayed on the gangway until all the boys were off the ship. A later drawing by Lance Calkin, published in the Christmas 1898 issue of *The Graphic*, shows Bourchier being urged by a trainee called Mudkin to leave the blazing *Goliath* – 'No, my boy,' says the caption. 'I have to be last. That's the way at sea.' In the end Bourchier left on the final boat to pull away from the side of the burning ship, the *Arethusa*'s galley. Bourchier posed for the drawing, the vessel in the background being the *Goliath*'s replacement, the first *Exmouth*.

The discipline of the boys and the courage of the ship's officers had undoubtedly saved many lives. As it was, one schoolmaster – Mr Wheeler from the King Alfred Training College in Winchester – was drowned along with seventeen boys. Considering the severity of the fire, the almost gale-force wind and the icy condition of the river, it was a relatively light toll. The inquest recorded a verdict of accidental death on those who had not survived and the Captain, crew and boys were congratulated on their conduct. Capt Bourchier went on to command the *Exmouth*, retiring in 1902. However, of Robert Loeber, the boy who inadvertently begun the disaster, nothing is known. He simply vanished into obscurity.

Just two weeks after the *Goliath* was destroyed, a similar disaster struck the Marine Society ship, *Warspite*. On the morning of 3 January 1876 she too was burned out as she lay at her moorings. Fire was reported to the Seamanship Instructor, Mr Webber, at about 1 a.m. and Capt Phipps, who was sleeping ashore

Boys learning to sew and mend on board the *Wellesley*.

that night, was hastily summoned back to the ship. Despite the rapid appearance of fire-fighting boats and wagons it soon became clear that the fire had gained too great a hold. Within a few hours the complete lower half of the ship was a mass of flames and, to the hundreds of spectators who had rushed to the riverbank to watch, it was clear that she could not be saved. On 8 January 1876, an eyewitness wrote in the *Kentish Independent*: 'We saw a spectacle which, for grandeur, could not be exceeded. The crater of the volcano into which we had been peering on deck, was now laid open to view. The broad stem was burnt away and we could see the roaring, raging fire which was consuming the bowels of the ship.'[101]

The braver – or more foolhardy – of the spectators hired small boats to take them alongside the doomed ship for a better view but once debris and, eventually, the masts began to topple they gave the *Warspite* a clean berth. The ship finally sank at her moorings and the rising tide extinguished the last of the flames.

For a while there was some concern about Nep, the pet dog of Capt Phipps and a great favourite of boys and public alike. Although the Captain had been ashore when the fire broke out the dog was onboard from the beginning to the end of the disaster. By good luck Nep was taken off when the *Warspite* was abandoned but rather than go with everyone else to the Woolwich Union Workhouse, where the boys were put up, he ran home and, at daybreak, was found sleeping across the Captain's doorstep.

To begin with it seemed that there was evidence of arson. A boy named Cotton claimed to have seen two unknown boys running away from the cockpit near the coal store where the fire began but others, who originally supported his claim, soon withdrew their evidence. Whether or not the 'running boys' actually existed

The *Wellesley* was burned out on 11 March 1914, the disaster being captured by enterprising local photographers.

was never proved but Cotton's description of them as 'old boys as the blue had washed out of their collars' certainly smacks of the truth. But he could equally as well have been lying in order to protect himself.[102]

Much to their annoyance, in the wake of the accident the Marine Society had to admit that the ship was not insured. Following the *Goliath* fire it was something they were planning to do but, in the end, events forestalled them. On 5 February 1876, a public meeting was held at the Mansion House to launch an appeal fund for a new ship and within a few months the Admiralty had agreed to loan the *Conqueror*.

Renamed *Warspite*, she served on the Thames for forty-one years until she, too, was destroyed by fire. This time it was clearly a case of arson and three boys were convicted of the offence – the story of that disaster has already been told in the first chapter of this book.

An arson attack also destroyed the Scottish Industrial School Ship, *Cumberland*, at Helensburgh on 18 February 1889. There were 390 boys and staff on board at the time. Officers and a volunteer party of fifty boys manned the three pumps, pouring water into the flames until everyone else had left the vessel. Then, seeing that the task was hopeless, they too abandoned ship. Boys were temporarily housed on the training brig *Cambria* until a replacement ship could be found. The *Cumberland* was valued at £27,000 but the committee at once set about fund-raising and attempting to find a new ship. This they succeeded in doing, the *Empress* – formerly the *Revenge*, flagship at Queenstown in Ireland – replacing her the same year.

Boys of the reformatory ship *Clarence*, *c.* 1890 – she was destroyed by fire in July 1899.

The *Wellesley* was yet another industrial ship destroyed by fire, being burned out on 11 March 1914. The cause of the fire remains unknown but all the boys and staff managed to get off before the blaze totally destroyed the ship. The bravery of one boy was noted in the local press and in newspapers as far away as New York when he ran through the smoke filled decks to rescue the baby of the Captain Superintendent from the stern cabin. Perfect discipline from the boys helped save the situation.

Being moored so close to North Shields the fire created much interest in the local population. Enterprising photographers soon took to the river in boats and, as a result, the *Wellesley* fire is one of the few wooden wall disasters to be captured on film. After the fire the boys were housed in the Tynemouth Palace until the end of the First World War. An appeal fund raised £22,000 for a replacement ship but the committee decided that shore-based training was a far safer option and the money was used to take over the old submarine base at Blyth. In 1933, the *Wellesley* became an approved school although it continued to send boys into the Merchant Navy for many years. It became a 'community home with education' in 1973 before finally closing its doors for good on 6 November 2006.

Perhaps the saddest or, at least, the most unfortunate of the training ship burnings concerned the Catholic reformatory ship, *Clarence*, on the Mersey – not once but twice was she burned to the water-line. The first disaster came on the afternoon of 17 January 1884 when fire was discovered on the lower deck at about 1.30 p.m. The seat of the fire was forward, almost in the bows of the ship and near to where oilcans had been stowed, and the crew were beaten back by the severity of the flames when they tried to reach it. Despite the frantic efforts of officials from the Liverpool Dock Board the fire gained such a hold that it quickly became apparent the ship was doomed. At times flames shot thirty feet into the air and, for a while, a degree of panic prevailed. Some boys got into the ship's boats and rowed about in disorder before the crew were able to re-establish control. That evening's *Liverpool Echo*, on the news-stands even as the fire raged, stated, 'the flames are spreading so rapidly that it has been deemed advisable to remove the boys and officials. At the time of writing two Rock Ferry steamers are alongside taking off the boys.'[103]

As the news of the fire spread, a number of relatives of the boys flocked to the landing stage in Liverpool and crossed to Rock Ferry in order to hear more news about their children. The boys were safe but the ship was clearly doomed. At 10 a.m. the following day the fire was still raging. Then, just after noon, when attempts to sink her by cannon shots fired from the dock tender, *Albert*, had failed, she was rammed and sunk by a steamer from the Upper Mersey Trust. Even then it took two collisions before the *Clarence* finally turned onto her side and settled below the waves.

The boys spent the next two nights on board the steamer *Gypsy Queen* before being housed in a brand new sanitary hospital at Bebington where a group of them were overheard talking amongst themselves, implying that the *Clarence* had been deliberately set on fire. The *Clarence* boys had recently earned themselves an unenviable reputation – only two years before a boy had been caught and charged with trying to burn her, while in September 1882 there was a mutiny on board that resulted in several of the ringleaders being sent to prison.[104]

As a result of the overheard conversation the police were brought in and six boys were taken into custody. Only the night before sixteen other boys had absconded from the sanitary hospital, taking advantage of the sudden space and lax control, and a reward was now posted for their recapture. Several of them, it was believed, were concerned in the arson attack. On 2 February 1884, seven *Clarence* boys aged between fourteen and seventeen appeared in court charged with setting fire to the ship. Among them were Edward Ryan, John Lloyd, Martin Mannion and Christopher Sewell. Edward Ryan, one of the absconders, stated: 'I asked Lloyd if he would set fire to the ship and he said "Yes, the first chance I get and we will do it." I then asked Mannion if he would do it and he said "Yes." So I then asked Sewell for some oil, and told him what it was for . . . He did afterwards give me a lamp full and I put it down the hold of the main hatch until we were ready to set it on fire.'[105] When they were ready Mannion struck the match and lit some old ropes onto which they had poured the oil. The ship went up like a tinderbox. At the time of the fire there were 216 boys and seven officers on board but, luckily, there were no fatalities. All seven of the accused were found guilty and each sentenced to five years penal servitude.

Understandably, the Admiralty was not over-keen to loan the *Clarence* Committee a new ship but after much discussion and debate with insurance companies a new vessel was finally offered. She was the 120-gun *Royal William*, which was

The battered hull of Nelson's *Foudroyant*, lying on the sands at Blackpool in July 1897.

renamed *Clarence* and moored in the Mersey in November 1885. A new captain superintendent, E. P. Statham, was appointed but the boys promptly challenged his authority by mutinying. For a while things were out of control with helpers from the shore having their boats capsized when the mutineers hurled down the ship's whalers and launches on top of them. Order was eventually restored but not before the Head Schoolmaster, Frederick Potter, was stabbed and so seriously wounded that he nearly died from his injuries. In the end, Captain Statham had to threaten the boys with a pistol – for which, incidentally, he had no ammunition – and the riot subsided. Thirteen of the ringleaders were sent to the Assizes.

The second *Clarence* fire took place on Wednesday 26 July 1899, the fire being discovered at 2 a.m. in the ship's lower hold. The Mersey steamers, *Firefly* and *Vigilant*, immediately stood by and sent across hoses, while the *Clarence* lowered her boats and 235 boys, along with Capt Yonge's wife, children and a female cook, were taken off. Bishop Allen of Shrewsbury happened to be on board that night as he had come to confirm twenty-four boys the following day and he too left the ship at this point, greatly impressed by the discipline and the courage of the youngsters. Despite everyone's efforts the fire quickly took hold and was soon out of control. At 6 a.m., just four hours after it had been first discovered, the *Clarence* broke in two, one half sinking quickly, the other half remaining afloat for some time, a mass of burning wood and spars.

Smoke had been one of the main problems, the wooden hull filling with a dense mass of grey mist that choked boys and staff alike. When combined with the flames it was a lethal combination. At about 5 a.m. the fire reached its culmination. Until then it had been mainly smoke that had caused the problems, but in the half-light of early morning the flames burst out with a force and a ferocity that startled everyone. 'Quickly devouring the wooden structures on deck, the flames reached the masts and rigging, which they seemed to swallow up as though they were but frail pieces of matchwood.'[106]

Above: The *Conway*, ashore in the Menai Straits, April 1953.

Left: Helpless and already doomed, the *Conway* is stranded and forlorn in this 1950s postcard view.

The *Cornwall*, beached and battered, off Gravesend, July 1948 – Port of London salvage vessels are in attendance.

Despite the initial protestations of Capt Yonge, arson was soon suspected. The officer on the middle watch admitted to smelling fire – as if someone was smoking tobacco – and a few moments later it became more pronounced. Then the blaze was discovered. When the matter was investigated it transpired that a number of boys had spent weeks carrying waste material such as bundles of old rags down to the bowels of the ship. They deliberately planned their attack for the very night that Bishop Allen was on board.

Following this second disastrous fire, the Catholic Reformatory Association quickly decided they had finished with water-borne reformatories. They still believed in the value of nautical training but, in future, they would offer such training on dry land and so they established St Aidan's Nautical School at Farnworth near Widnes, a reformatory that continued to run until 1981.[107]

It was not just fire that caused the end of many wooden training ships. Two of them were wrecked on the dangerous coast of Britain.

When Joseph Cobb rescued Nelson's *Foudroyant* from a firm of German ship-breakers at Swinemunde and brought her back to Erith for repairs, the ship was in a very poor state. It cost him a fortune to make her seaworthy, and in an effort to raise even more money to maintain her – according to Cobb she cost him £4,300 a year – he proposed running the *Foudroyant* as a training ship. But the money paid by the parents of the trainees only went so far. So he hit on the plan of sailing the old ship around the coast and opening her up to the public. The young boy trainees, aided by a minimal crew, would do the actual sailing.

After an initial opening in early June 1896 – admission two shillings, one shilling after 5 p.m. – *Foudroyant* began her progress around the British Isles. Twenty-one boys were undergoing training as she went, instructed by a crew of six qualified seamen. By 16 June the ship was off Blackpool, the plan being to head for the Isle of Man, then double back and lay up for the winter in Milford Haven. Unfortunately, that night a terrible storm blew up and *Foudroyant*, in full view of thousands of fascinated spectators on the promenade, was thrown up onto Blackpool beach.

The Blackpool lifeboat affected a successful and dangerous rescue but it took time to alert the crew and get alongside the old wooden wall. This meant that 'for six hours the boys sheltered under the poop and sang songs while, all around them, the ship was breaking up under the force of the sea.'[108]

It must have been a terrifying ordeal for the youngsters, some as young as thirteen and fourteen, but they held their nerve and never faltered while waiting for the lifeboat. The *Foudroyant* was a total wreck and at low tide the next day people were able to walk around the remains. So accessible was she that there was much looting from the wreck. Her figurehead and some of her cannon were salvaged, the figurehead going to Joseph Cobb's home at Caldicot Castle, the guns to the docks at Milford Haven.

As described elsewhere, the *Foudroyant* was soon replaced with another vessel. The original ship was broken up where she lay on the beach at Blackpool – a sad end for such a historic vessel.

The other training ship to be wrecked was the *Conway*. Moved from the Mersey in 1941, the vessel lay off Bangor in the Menai Straits for several years. However, by 1949, the accommodation on board was inadequate and an arrangement was made with the Marquess of Anglesey to use part of his house at Plas Newydd as a shore base. In April that year the *Conway* was towed to a new location, just off Plas Newydd: 'It was a short but difficult journey through the treacherous Swillies Channel and one which could be undertaken only on the highest tide of the year. But it was successfully accomplished.'[109] Four years later the ship was in clear need of a refit. The Mercantile Marine Service Association planned to continue using her for at least another two or three decades, so it was essential that she should be kept in working order. The plan was to tow her to Cammel Laird's dry dock at Birkenhead but, in order to negotiate the Swillies, the tow had to be carried out on the high spring tide. Even then the clearance between the Devil's Teeth Rocks would be, at best, just four feet.

The sad end of a proud ship. The bombed *Cornwall* in her last days.

The journey began early in the morning on Tuesday 14 April 1953, the *Conway* being towed by two Liverpool tugs, *Dongarth* and *Minegarth*, one at the bow and the other on the stern. All went well and the *Conway* was soon through the most difficult part of the Swillies between the Britannia Railway Bridge and the suspension bridge. There the little flotilla was met by the flood tide.

Estimation of the flood tide was at five knots but, unfortunately, a sudden north-westerly wind almost doubled its force and the tugs, only capable of ten knots at most, were not able to make headway. The after-tug came around to join the forward one and a line was stretched between the vessels. Unfortunately, the hawser parted and the *Conway*'s bows swung round towards the Caernarfonshire shore. Before the horrified gaze of thousands of spectators, the ship ran hard ashore. An inspection by salvage officers at low water quickly revealed that the *Conway*'s hull was badly buckled and strained and there was little hope of refloating her. At the next high tide the ship flooded aft and, almost before people knew, her back had broken. The old ship was declared a total loss and lay for some time on the foreshore, a curious and fascinating sight for onlookers, before she was finally broken up where she lay. Her remains were finally destroyed by fire in October 1956.[110]

In the wake of the disaster Capt Eric Hewitt, the captain superintendent, was much criticised. He had been on board the *Conway* at the time of the wreck but because she was classified as a hulk with no motive power he had no responsibility for the tow. Hewitt, knowing the strength of the current, had asked for three tugs but was told that the final authority lay with the towing master and that two were considered more than enough for the job.

The *Cornwall* had been operating since 1859 as a reformatory school ship, first at Purfleet and then, after 1926, at Denton, just below Gravesend. It was a lonely mooring at Denton, the only other vessels in the area being barges loaded with explosives. Despite this, however, by 1927 all school instruction was carried out on shore, the old wooden wall being used solely for instruction in seamanship and for accommodation.[111]

Inspections during the 1930s had become increasingly critical of the regime and of the curriculum being offered on the *Cornwall* and there were serious doubts about the viability of the establishment. By 1939 the ship was in a poor state, and the rotten mainmast had to be hoisted out of the vessel. In July of that year a decision was taken that the ship should close, although, because of the boys still on board, the earliest possible closure date was March 1941. Then, in the summer of 1939, war was declared against Germany. The *Cornwall* boys were immediately evacuated to a Ministry of Labour camp at Brandon in Suffolk, but due to the strange circumstances, and what many of the lads perceived as greater freedom, discipline broke down. Within a very short space of time they were licensed off and the establishment was closed down.

Meanwhile, the ship herself still lay off Denton. Despite the fact that the reformatory had already dispersed its pupils and closed, there remained various problems, notably a debt – £1,800 was still owed on a loan that had been taken out in 1938 to renew the upper deck – and that had to be cleared before the ship could be returned to the Admiralty.[112]

When the German Blitz began in earnest, the *Cornwall* was one of the earliest victims. During these troubled months Gravesend was bombed several times and during one raid in September 1940 there was a direct hit on the *Cornwall*, causing severe damage and effectively finishing her for any further use. The battered hull was simply towed ashore and left to rot. She lay on the riverbank for the duration of the war, finally being broken up where she lay in the late 1940s.

Fire and shipwreck were occupational hazards for sailors in the days of wooden ships. Along with a German bomb or two, they were instrumental in ending the careers of several training ships. They were not alone, however. Many factors contributed to the final demise of a system that had survived for centuries but, as the twentieth century wore on, seemed increasingly out of step with modern life and the requirements of both the Royal and Merchant Navies.

CHAPTER ELEVEN
Scandal and Disaster, Death, Mutiny and Riot

Scandal dogged many of the training ships, particularly the reformatory and industrial schools, almost from the beginning of their careers. Mass communication was in its infancy in the nineteenth and early twentieth centuries but, even so, the Victorian and Edwardian public were as fascinated with scandal and mischief as their modern counterparts. In particular, the newly enfranchised middle classes – the young bank clerks and shop managers, the postal workers and schoolteachers – gleefully devoured the news of riot, mutiny and shipwreck as they sat over their morning coffee and breakfast rolls.

Probably the most famous of these public outrages was the *Akbar* Affair, a scandalous series of events that the newspaper entrepreneur, Horatio Bottomley, took up with gusto. It was a story that held the people of Britain in thrall for many months during 1910 and 1911.

On 22 October 1910 Bottomley's scandal sheet, the *John Bull*, carried an article under the headline 'Reformatory School Horrors – How Boys at the *Akbar* School are Tortured – Several Deaths'. According to *John Bull*, the paper had been contacted by Ronald Adams, lately deputy superintendent of the school, stating that he and his wife, the matron, had resigned their positions because they were sickened by the barbarity of the regime. Floggings, it was claimed, were public affairs, boys being gagged by having blankets wrapped around their mouths and then held across trestles and caned until they bled. The canes used were branches from hawthorn trees, the birch rods wrapping themselves around the bodies or thighs of the boys every time a blow was landed. Other punishments included being drenched with freezing water and kept standing up all night. Several deaths, it was said, had resulted from such treatment.[113]

John Bull did not just make allegations, it also provided evidence and went on to quote an ex-staff member of the *Akbar* who spoke about the death of a boy named Brown. The boy had complained about being cold and ill and the member of staff concerned had ordered him to report sick. It was not to be. 'At 5.00 p.m., passing the first bathroom, I heard piercing screams from inside . . . The bathroom was in darkness but I could just discern that two boys were pouring cold water over Brown who was naked. The boys then stopped, and commenced to dress him

T.S. "WARSPITE": DAILY ROUTINE.

A.M.

0550	Turn out early Washers, Buglers and Hammock Stowers.
0600	Reveille. Lash up and Stow. Hands to wash.
0630	Assembly. Hang up Towels.
0635	Scrub and wash up Upper Deck.
0700	Cleaning Stations. Clean Mess Deck and Boats.
0735	Breakfast.
0800	Sick Bay Call.
0820	Band Call.
0825	Officers' Call.
0830	Divisions. Prayers.
	March off to Instructions and School.
1030	Stand Easy.
1045	Carry on.
1130	Request Boys and Defaulters.
1230	Return Stores.
1235	Cooks.
1240	Dinner.

P.M.

1300	Cooks and Sweepers clear up Mess Deck.
1350	"G."
1352	Officers' Call.
1355	Assembly. March off to Instructions and School.
1455	Return Stores.
1500	Assembly. Physical Drill or Boat Pulling or Land to Field.
1605	Cooks.
1610	Tea.
1635	Cooks clear up Mess Deck. Cleaning Stations.
1645	Open Reading Room and Gymnasium.
1755	Close do. do. do.
1800	"Preparation" Instruction.
1845	Divisions Muster and Wash.
1920	Cooks.
1925	Supper.
1940	Muster for Tooth Cleaning Parade.
1955	Stand by Hammock.
2030	Evening Muster. Prayers. Boys turn in.

1500—1600 in Winter : Sports, Recreation, etc.

1500—1600 in Summer : Boat Pulling, Signals etc.

Left: The Daily Routine on the Marine Society's *Warspite* – a similar routine was followed on all the training ships.

Below: Boys row out to the *Clio* – an episode of thieving on board the ship made Captain Monger despair in 1881.

They all seem well fed, content and happy in this shot of boys on the *Cornwall* but there were two serious assaults on staff within a few years of this photograph being taken.

... I did not see the boy again until 6.00 p.m. Then I saw two boys dragging him across the yard. He was in a state of collapse – could not walk or speak ... I was informed by a boy at 6.45 p.m. that he was dead.'[114]

The paper quoted another brutal death, that of a boy who had soiled himself. He, too, was given the water treatment and left to stand in his drenched clothes. Despite being found and scrubbed dry by the matron the boy subsequently died. The coroner at the inquest severely censured the officer responsible but the man was still employed at the school and the committee had held no investigation.

As a result of *John Bull's* articles the Home Secretary – none other than Winston Churchill – was forced to order a full inquiry. He appointed C. F. G. Masterman, Under Secretary of State, to lead the investigation. Capt Beuttler, the captain superintendent and others concerned were not suspended from duty and when, in March 1911, the report was presented all charges of brutality were rejected. It was acknowledged that irregular punishments had taken place but the inquiry accepted Beuttler's explanation that he had had blankets held to the faces of boys being caned solely to prevent their cries disturbing passers-by on the tow path outside! *John Bull* was, understandably, incensed and accusations of a 'whitewash' were liberally flung around.

On 14 May 1911, over 7,000 people took part in a public protest meeting about the affair and in the elections of that year the government inquiry became one of the central issues. As a direct result of the *Akbar* Affair, Churchill was forced to appoint a departmental committee to look at the constitution, management, discipline and education in reformatory and industrial schools. The issue was simple – which came first, the school or the child?

Debate continued to rumble on, the *Daily Mail* publishing a series of articles under the banner headline 'Schools for Crime'. The reformatories were strongly attacked for a variety of reasons, not least because of the brutal nature of their regimes. Although delayed by the First World War and its consequences, the *Akbar* Affair did eventually lead to a total revamping of the system of education for young offenders, to the replacing of reformatories by approved schools and to greater government control in their management and direction – exactly what Mary Carpenter had been advocating in the 1850s.[115]

The *Akbar* Affair actually took place when the ship had moved ashore, to premises at Heswall on the Wirral, but the old wooden wall was no stranger to disaster and confusion either. Attempts at escape from the ship were common, so much so that a bounty of twenty shillings a head was offered on all absconders. It was a difficult and dangerous business trying to swim or row almost half a mile to shore before the alarm was given, but barely a month went by without somebody trying to get away. Several boys drowned or were swept out to sea in the attempt.

On 12 August 1889 two boys, known in the records simply as Fishwick and Thorn, leapt over the side in a bid for freedom. Half-way to shore Thorn found himself in difficulties and, treading water, Fishwick passed across the cork lifebelt he was wearing. As he was desperately trying to pull it on Thorn sank out of sight below the waves. He never surfaced and his body was later found floating face down in the river. Fishwick was arrested in Liverpool later the same day, returned to the *Akbar* and punished by eighteen strokes of the cane and a day in the cells.

Being what they were, stationary vessels anchored half a mile or so off shore, all training ships found themselves in potentially hazardous situations. When the gale-force winds of winter and early spring lashed the waters of the Mersey into a frenzy, they caused serious problems for ships like the *Akbar*.

In March 1884, one of the *Akbar* boats, containing twelve boys, two officers and a boy visitor by the name of Duckworth – who had come aboard to see his brother – was caught in a sudden storm. Despite struggling against the ferocious winds, with eight of the twelve oars broken or lost over the side, the boat was carried up river and, four hours later, thrown up onto the desolate mud of Frodsham Marsh. Wading chest high through the water the party managed to get ashore, frozen and starving. By now night had fallen and it was impossible to get off the marsh. For ten hours the boys and their officers endured hail, rain and wind before dawn broke and the chief officer was at last able to find assistance. The only fatality was the boy Duckworth who had become separated during the night and was later found dead from exposure.

If the *Akbar* boys narrowly escaped total disaster in 1884, the *Cornwall* was not so lucky some years later. On 30 August 1915 sixteen boys and one officer, Mr Edward Francis Lane, were drowned when their cutter, the *Alert*, was in a collision with the steam tug *Empress* off Purfleet. At the funeral of the boys and Mr Lane some 3,000 people attended and walked in the procession that stretched for a full mile along the road.

It was not just the elements that caused problems. Mutiny broke out on the *Akbar* on 25 September 1887. Capt Symons was on leave at the time and the ship was under the temporary control of the chief officer, Mr Callender. Boys suddenly downed their tools and refused to work, then ran through the ship urging others to join them. Armed with sticks and belaying pins the boys forced the officers back before breaking down the storeroom door and helping themselves to clothes and other items. They also broke into the Captain's cabin, stealing his wife's jewellery. They then took one of the *Akbar*'s boats and rowed off towards Liverpool. The two ringleaders were later arrested and charged – both of them received three months hard labour – and were refused re-admission to the *Akbar*.[116]

The atmosphere on the *Akbar* was always tense and fraught with danger. A few years after the 1887 mutiny, in August 1892, the Captain went to the sleeping deck at about 10 p.m. He found a great deal of whistling and catcalling, behaviours the Chief Officer could not stop. Apparently it had been going on for almost an hour. As soon as the Captain appeared the noise stopped but recommenced the moment he left. The noises stopped as the boys drifted off to sleep but began again at 6.45 a.m. The Captain immediately cancelled all leave and summoned everyone to the upper deck where he had them stand at attention for two hours. After that boys went off quietly to their workstations.

At lunchtime the Captain was approached by two petty officers who reported that there would be no more noise – as long as leave was reinstated. Once more the boys were summoned and this time they were informed that there would be no bartering or coming to terms. Leave would be stopped for as long as the Captain saw fit. Staff were armed in case of trouble but the boys knew when they were beaten and the behaviour disappeared as quickly as it had come.

Most of the other reformatory and industrial ships experienced similar events. In 1895, a complaint from a schoolmaster on the *Wellesley* said that boys thought guilty of masturbation had their genitals painted with a blistering liquid. In the subsequent inquiry a number of irregularities were discovered, including the use of boys to find prostitutes and drink for the crew during the absence of the Captain Superintendent.[117]

The behaviour of boys on the *Clio* during the year 1881 had, according to the Inspector of Reformatory and Industrial Schools, left a lot to be desired. Apparently they broke into a cabin and the provisions store and there were numerous cases of lying, petty theft, disobedience and bad language. It prompted Captain Monger of the ship to ask that 'if the parents or guardians, brothers, sisters, cousins, uncles and aunts of these boys are not able (with all the power and love they possess) to control one child, how can we be expected to control two or three hundred if our hands are tied, as some people would wish to tie them?'[118]

The absence of the captain superintendents – or, sometimes, their ineffectiveness – seems to have been a common factor in many of these outbreaks. On the *Mars* there was an attempted arson attack during the absence of Capt Scott and a number of boys who were cruising on the tender, *Francis Mollison*. It was May 1883 and there were 340 boys on board. At 3.30 in the morning an officer saw flames coming from the Captain's cabin, shooting up around the mizzenmast. Bucket chains were quickly formed and with the boys taken ashore the fire was out by 7 a.m. Three culprits were discovered, arrested, flogged and sent off to reformatories.[119]

On the *Cornwall* there was a much more serious turn of events. Late in 1902 Capt Williams took command and found the ship in a very unsatisfactory condition, probably due to the illness and failing powers of his predecessor, Adml Morrell. Williams had to weed out several of the officers who were unsuitable and ineffective, and while this was undoubtedly necessary, it did lead to a feeling of unease on the ship. At the end of June 1903 Capt Williams noticed that many of the boys seemed particularly unsettled. Fearing a possible mutiny, he assembled the entire crew on deck and asked for anyone who had a grievance to come forward – twenty boys immediately presented themselves. Their complaint was that they were being watched by one of the officers but once they had voiced their concerns and were told that the man was only doing his duty, Williams felt that the potentially explosive situation had eased.

Within a day or so, however, one of the seaman instructors, Mr Maine, reported a boy called Bennett for lying. Before the boy could be seen by the Captain-Superintendent things escalated out of hand, as Williams later explained in a letter to the Home Office: 'I very much regret to report that two of the lads (3426 C. Bennett and 3594 A. Flack) under detention . . . were yesterday morning, the 29th inst., guilty of a dastardly attack on one of the officers (Mr Maine, Seaman Instructor).'[120] At breakfast, when Maine was in charge of the mess deck, the two boys had waited until he was not looking and then leapt out of their seats, each of them stabbing him in the back. Several boys were also implicated and, for punishment, Bennett, Flack and four others were each given eighteen strokes with the birch. When the Reformatory Schools Inspector, J. Granville Legge, arrived on board the *Cornwall* to investigate the incident the following day, he found Mr Maine relatively happy and the ship in a calm state. The wounded man did not want the boys prosecuted but rather than risk reprisals or a repetition several of them were quickly moved off the ship to the reformatory at Redhill.

The stabbing was the second attack on an officer on board the *Cornwall*. Only twelve months earlier, during the unsettled period of Adml Morrell's illness, a far more serious stabbing had occurred when two boys, Percival and Rixon, knifed the ship's second officer while he was walking on the afterdeck. They, along with three others who had sharpened the knives, were quickly arrested and brought to court. *The Eastern Daily Press* reported on the trial: 'certain boys who were proved to be delinquents were ordered to be punished. Some of them, resenting this, put their heads together and arranged that when they went out with one of the officers they would throw him overboard. However, they did not go out and they turned their attention to Henry Hunt, the second officer, and it was alleged that one of the prisoners stabbed him in the back with a knife.'[121]

The real motive behind the attack was a raid that the boys had made on the ship's storeroom a few days before, stealing cans of corned beef – they feared that the officers were close to discovering who had carried out the theft. Hunt was seriously injured in the affair but he recovered. The boys pleaded guilty and asked for a second chance – amazingly, they were returned to the ship.

As if the two stabbings weren't enough, in May 1903 the *Cornwall* was the centre of yet another scandal. This time the problem was blankets. In a short but succinct leader article on 21 May, the *Daily Mail* cut to the core of the problem: 'Eleven boys have been

Despite the idyllic nature of this drawing by Louis Wain, showing boys shortening the cable on the *Mercury* (it was a generic view as there are other examples of the same picture with names like *Cornwall* on the boys hats), there were many instances of bullying on board the training ships.

stricken down with enteric on board the Reformatory Ship *Cornwall* lying off Purfleet as the result of sleeping in fever-infested blankets brought from South Africa.'[122]

Five hundred blankets had been bought from the War Office by Capt Williams, with the full approval of the committee. The blankets had recently been brought back to Britain after the end of the Boer War but, unfortunately, they were in a filthy condition, stained with blood and swarming with typhoid bacilli. The most disturbing element of the scandal was not the fact that filthy blankets could be sold but, rather, that the Captain and committee could issue them to the *Cornwall* boys without them being washed or cleaned in any way.

The Home Office was often off-hand in its response to problems such as the *Cornwall* blankets. When the Medical Officer to the *Clio* drew attention to the fact that several boys were suffering from inflammation of the knee joint caused by kneeling to wash and scrub the decks, he was met with virtual indifference. The Home Office comment was simply that 'the danger of the complaint can be obviated to a large extent but it is, I believe, quite common for sailors to kneel down when scrubbing decks, and the boys will have to become inured to it.'[123]

Bullying was a constant factor on all the training ships. Even on the two officer ships, *Conway* and *Worcester*, new trainees were subjected to brutal treatment from the older boys and it was many years before *Britannia* at Dartmouth was able to reduce the level of intimidation. On *Ganges*, *Arethusa* and other vessels such bullying was often tolerated by staff, being seen as good for the character.

Staff regularly used peer-pressure to control youngsters and when boys were given such power it became a terrible weapon.

In his novel about life in a nautically-based approved school, Bill Meilem caught the mood and attitude quite perfectly: 'Dando heard loud and clear, and knew the warning for what it meant. There was to be high jinks in the Division when he got back. He'd seen it all before. With Creegan. Creegan had absconded. When he got back the Division had given him high jinks. Individually, the members of the Division were nothing – just boys. But together, with Petty Officer Mundy goading them, the Division became an animal, a terrible animal . . . After the fists and boots and the wooden slats from the beds there had been worse for Creegan. The Division had thrown him from the landing down into the stairwell, carried away by the power of the throng. Creegan would never walk properly again. Not with that busted pelvis.'[124]

Sometimes bullying reached unacceptable levels. On 9 February 1906, at Bangor Infirmary, William Crooks, a thirteen-year-old trainee on the *Clio*, died from concussion to the brain, a condition caused by repeated beatings. The ship's officers had seen nothing and only noticed the condition of the boy when they went ashore for recreation. Crooks complained of feeling faint and could hardly walk. Taken to the sickbay, bruises were discovered on his body and he admitted that two boys had knocked him down and kicked him as he lay on the floor. The next day Crooks slipped into a coma and, despite being admitted to the infirmary, died soon afterwards. The boy's injuries had been sustained from a prolonged episode of bullying by two boys, one of whom was called Singleton, who clearly took pleasure in using their strength against a weaker and smaller boy.

At the coroner's inquest boys from the *Clio* were called as witnesses. One of them, Christopher Norton, reported that 'last Sunday morning he saw Singleton knocking Crooks about. Every time Crooks stood up Singleton knocked him down by jabbing both his fists into Crooks' chest. There were a lot of boys around at the time but no one interfered with Singleton who kept on doing it. Crooks fell onto his back every time he was knocked down.'[125]

The jury, however, returned a verdict of 'Death by Misadventure'. The Home Office Inspector, J. G. Legge, felt that while the jury had taken a lenient view he was in agreement with Capt Supdt Langdon that it was a case of bullying, no more, and that the situation was not altered by the fact that Crooks was a boy of more delicate build than most others and, therefore, more likely to succumb to injuries that other boys would have soon got over. Besides, the two bullies had been birched – that was punishment enough.[126]

Legge did recommend, however, that the managers of the training ships should try to find a higher class of seaman instructor in order to stop things like this happening again. So maybe some good did come out of Crooks death, even though the boy himself was long past any useful human help.

The inherent dangers of fire, bullying, death and mutiny finally went a long way towards ending the process of training boys on board ship. It took some time but, for those who were aware, the writing was on the wall before the end of the nineteenth century. The system was already dead – the trouble was, the system did not know it.

CHAPTER TWELVE
The End of the Road

Training ships were not just a British phenomenon. Many countries used sailing vessels to help educate their sailors during the nineteenth and early twentieth centuries. As early as 1866 the government of New South Wales moored the *Vernon* in Sydney Harbour, the ship acting both as a home and as a nautical school for delinquent boys. She was replaced by the *Sobraon* in 1890, the ship being taken over by the Royal Australian Navy as a training ship for men and boys of 'the lower deck' in 1911. Over the years France had many training ships, notably *Le Borda* and *La Bretagne*. Sweden had the *Freja* and the USA had vessels such as the *Constellation*, *Boxer* and *Hartford*.

Germany, of course, was a little different. The Prussian Navy only came into existence in 1853 when Frederick William IV agreed to the founding of a Prussian Admiralty. Initially, Prussian naval officers were trained in the navies of England, Holland, Denmark, Sweden and the USA, or they were hired from the German Mercantile Marine. Such a system could not last and eventually it was necessary to found a training school on board the corvette, *Amazone*. Unfortunately for the Germans she went down in a storm, drowning most of the cadets on board. Undaunted, Germany continued to expand her navy until, by the early years of the twentieth century, it was a real threat to Britain's naval supremacy.[127]

As far as Britain was concerned, when the twentieth century opened the need to train sailors and officers for the Royal and Merchant Navies remained strong. The country had always relied on its Merchant Marine to supply much of its economic needs – and on the all-powerful Royal Navy to keep the sea-lanes open and ensure that the country itself remained safe.

In 1913, the Fourth National Conference on Sea Training was held at County Hall, London. In his preface to the report, the Marquess of Lansdowne was clear about the value of nautical training: 'I have long been of the opinion that we ought to get hold of the boys of this country and give them, while they are still young and easily moulded, a training which will fit them to serve their country with efficiency by land or sea when they grow up. It is not necessary to insist upon the disciplinary and educative value of such training, a value which will, I believe, be found to exceed that of a great part of the learning which lads now acquire in State-supported schools.'[128]

The French training ship *La Bretagne*.

It was clear that in the years before the First World War there remained a belief in training boys for careers at sea. However, the style of such training had already begun to alter. Questions were already being asked about the value and the viability of accommodating enthusiastic and energetic young boys on wooden ships moored half a mile or so off the coast – surely it would be better, people said, to house them ashore where they could enjoy the space and freedom of playing fields and other leisure facilities. Outbreaks of fever on board ships like the *Cornwall* – rarely a year went by without two or three deaths on many or most of the training ships – had begun to make people think that maybe, just maybe, the old wooden walls were unhygienic. New purpose-built schools ashore were bound to be better for health.

Training of officers for the Royal Navy had come ashore once the new college at Dartmouth opened in 1905 and, while the two Merchant Navy officer ships remained in use, both the *Conway* and the *Worcester* had the run of extensive shore establishments. Closure of the *St Vincent* and the removal of boy seaman training from the ship *Ganges* to the new shore base at Shotley was another nail in the coffin for the training ships.

As far as the reformatory and industrial ships were concerned a similar train of thought was also in operation. A departmental committee on the schools was soon commenting: 'No ships in future to receive certificates as Reformatory and Industrial Schools, and nautical schools on land to be substituted, as opportunities offer, for the existing ships.'[129]

Several of the schools had already closed or moved ashore. The *Havannah*, old and out of touch with the realities of the moment, shut her doors for the last time in 1903. For many years the ship had sent almost no boys to sea and the point

The Cardiff Industrial School ship *Havannah*, surrounded by warehouses, is shown here in her final days.

had been reached where no amount of patching served to keep the old frigate's planking weather-tight. The Admiralty was not willing to offer another ship and the committee reluctantly came to the decision that it was in the interests of all for the school to close. The few remaining boys were transferred to the *Formidable* across the Channel at Portishead (along with capital investments to the tune of £5,000) and the hulk sold to Mr H. Norris, on the condition that he cleared the site within four months.

In 1901, the *Formidable* had also been found to be in bad condition. Her seams were leaking and in her exposed position off the Somerset coast things were only likely to get worse. At one stage the committee did ask permission to move the vessel into Portishead Dock but because of the increased amount of trade and commerce in the dock the request was refused. The ship had always been one of the most successful of the industrial schools and there was little desire to close, certainly not amongst the committee, not in the Home Office either. As a result it was decided to move the establishment ashore. With the help of Home Office funding, land was acquired and a superb new school was built overlooking the Bristol Channel, complete with dormitory bedrooms and extensive playing fields. The *Formidable* was towed away for breaking but the tender, *Polly*, was retained in order to give the boys practical experience of life afloat. The National Nautical School, as the new establishment was known, continued to run as an approved school and then as a community home until it closed in the 1980s.

The *Clarence* Committee had decided on shore-based training after the 1899 fire and the success of the new venture was not lost on the members of the Liverpool Reformatory Association. With the *Akbar*'s condition deteriorating

Lighthouse and National Nautical School, Portishead.   70844. J.V.

The new National Nautical School that replaced the *Formidable* on the banks of the Severn Estuary in 1905.

year by year it was apparent that something would have to be done about the old ship. By 1906 she was making a ton of water every twenty-four hours, through her side and bottom. The Captain reported that he did not consider it safe to rig the main sail again and there was a most unpleasant and unhealthy ooze from the ship's midst.[130]

New land-based premises were bought, and, on Monday 2 December 1907, the old *Akbar* was towed away to the breaker's yard. The school moved to Heswall on the Wirral where, despite the insistence of the Home Office that the new establishment should now be called the Heswall Nautical School, the place was always known, by boys and staff alike, as the *Akbar* until it finally closed in 1956.

There were initially 200 boys at the new school, a number that was eventually reduced to 120, and the premises included dormitories, two football fields, instruction huts and HMS *Moonshine*. This was a hollow concrete replica of a steam ship, made by the boys, in much the same way as mock ships had been created for use at Quarrier's Homes and at the Royal Hospital School in Greenwich. This one was different in that it was a replica of a steam ship, not a sailing one. Although there were classrooms inside the *Moonshine* most of the training actually took place in the nearby seamanship instruction huts.

Shaftesbury on the Thames was another school to close in the early years of the twentieth century. When the London County Council succeeded the London School Board they found the ship in need of extensive repair. Rather than spend huge sums of money on what they considered a risky operation, the LCC closed the school in 1905. The *Shaftesbury* was sold in May 1906 and broken up in Holland.

The end of the *Formidable*, the old ship being towed away for breaking.

The *Southampton* had endured a falling role for several years. It was symptomatic of many industrial schools in the early years of the twentieth century as children, reluctantly, became used to the idea of compulsory education and interventions other than residential care, such as the use of probation officers, became more widely employed for troublesome youngsters. By 1904, of the 11,000 boys admitted to industrial schools as a result of truancy – one of the prime reasons for admission – over half had been cured of their problem after one short spell of detention. Despite average attendance at English public elementary schools rising from 1,062,999 to 5,037,498 between 1869 and 1903, the committals of juvenile offenders under sixteen years of age fell from 10,314 in 1869 to just 1,119 in 1903.

With major problems about mooring the *Southampton* in an increasingly busy seaway, the future of the Hull Training Ship looked bleak. When, in 1911, the liner *Juno* ran into the old wooden wall, badly damaging her port bow and the moorings, the estimated cost of repairing the damage was over £1,000. The Home Office suggested that the committee might like to consider a move to a land-based school, but the cost of such a move would have been in the region of £25,000. The managers met and decided that they would resign the *Southampton*'s certificate as soon as boys could be transferred to other establishments. The certificate was formally resigned on 1 June 1912 and on 26 June the ship was sold to Messrs Hughes, Bolckow at Blyth for breaking up.[131]

After the *Warspite* fire of 1918 the move to shore-based training was exacerbated. Within a few years Devitt & Moore put an end to their ship-borne training scheme and, instead, concentrated their efforts on the new college at Pangbourne – much safer for all concerned, it was felt.

Christ's Hospital School had never been a sea-going establishment, despite being one of the earliest nautical schools in the world. The establishment had moved to a

An aerial view of the Heswall Nautical School, the land-based establishment that replaced the *Akbar* in 1907.

Boys of the *Wellesley* at Tynemouth Palace.

Above: Boys parade at the *Mercury*,
circa 1965 – the old ship can still be
seen in the background.

Right: The Royal Hospital School
moved to Holbrook in the 1930s.

The *Mars* is towed away for breaking up at Inverkeithing.

new, purpose-built school at West Horsham at the end of the nineteenth century, the foundation stone being laid on 23 October 1897. Special trains had to be laid on in order to get people there for the ceremony. The school is still running but, these days, as a public school and there is little or no connection with sea training.

The other early nautical school, the Royal Hospital School at Greenwich, also changed its location. In 1921, Gifford Sherman Reade donated the Holbrook Estate just outside Ipswich to the Admiralty for the exclusive benefit of Greenwich Hospital. The Duke of York laid the foundation stone for the new school building in 1928 and five years later the move was made from Greenwich to Holbrook. The school still runs, and is recognised as one of the premier independent schools in the country. The maritime heritage lives on at the school, all pupils being issued with a naval uniform that is still worn for formal public parades.[132]

The *Mercury* at Hamble had become something of a hybrid establishment in the years after the death of the founder, Charles Hoare. Under the control of C. B. Fry and his wife, Beatie Sumner, a punishing and brutal regime was created. Punishment fights in the boxing ring were a common occurrence, usually with two grossly mismatched youngsters. The one destined to lose had, in some way, offended Beatie and such an affair was usually greeted by total silence from the boys. If the bigger boy did not give the other a very bloody hammering he would undoubtedly be in the ring as the potential loser next time. Beatie would watch the fights, shouting 'Make him bleed, boy, make him bleed.'[133]

By the end of the Second World War all pretensions of training boys for careers at sea had gone. The *Mercury* was now running as a public school of sorts, but people in local government, with scholarships to dispense, were also sending the establishment boys who were in need of strong discipline, which was exactly what

The cruiser *Phaeton* replaced the original wooden wall *Indefatigable* during the First World War and continued to operate as a Training Ship on the Mersey until she was moved to the Menai Straits in 1940.

Beatie Sumner provided. Beatie's halcyon days, however, were almost ended. In April 1946 she fell and broke her hip, dying shortly afterwards, and C. B. Fry did not outlive her by long. Almost immediately routines and regimes began to change. The curriculum was broadened, and by the time Comdr R. F. Hoyle took charge in 1960, the place was effectively a minor public school, with the nautical ingredient reduced to no more than 25 per cent of the total curriculum. By the end of the 1960s, however, the school was uneconomic and out of date. The *Mercury* duly closed in 1968, Earl Mountbatten of Burma presiding over the closing ceremonies.

With the decline in the British Merchant shipping in the years immediately after the First World War, several of the industrial school ships soon found themselves struggling to survive. They were, perhaps, the most vulnerable of all the training ships, their clientele usually being the least willing both to accept discipline and to learn the intricacies of the profession. Their whole purpose had been to place boys into positions on board ship, a task they carried out with greater or lesser degrees of success. Now, however, there was virtually no Merchant Navy to take their boys. It was not the only problem.

With their ships gradually wearing out and the general consensus that, when the time came, training should be transferred from ship to shore bases, the industrial schools found themselves in a dilemma that was often solved in only one way. Faced by the prospect of having to find a huge sum of money to build a land-based school to replace the old corvette, the *Clio* reluctantly closed in May 1919, while the *Mount Edgcumbe* followed suit in June the following year. The *Empress* at Helensburgh also closed, on 16 March 1923.

Arethusa boys march on the deck of their ship, headed by their band.

When the managers of the *Mars* resigned the ship's certificate in 1929, the wooden wall was towed away for breaking. The ship-breakers, however, soon encountered more than they bargained for. Oxyacetylene burners and guillotine shears, so effective on the iron and steel of modern ships, proved useless against the massive oak timbers of the *Mars*. Her sides were, in places, thirty-two inches thick and attempts to drive in a three-inch nail resulted in the nail bending without making any sort of entry. In the end explosives were used to blow the old ship apart.

The voluntary or charity ships struggled on for some time. The cruiser, *Phaeton*, had replaced the wooden *Indefatigable* during the First World War and in these slightly more salubrious surroundings the establishment continued offering a service on the Mersey during the inter-war years. The *Phaeton*, renamed *Indefatigable*, was moved from the Mersey to the Menai Straits in 1941 and a few years later, in 1944, the boys came ashore to land accommodation purchased from the Marquess of Anglesey at Plas Menai. The old cruiser was towed away for scrapping. Over the years there was less and less nautical education provided at the school, which increasingly operated as a public school until its eventual closure in 1994.

After the wreck of the *Conway* in 1953, the establishment operated from a shore base on Anglesey. The British Shipping Federation took responsibility for nautical training while Cheshire Education Authority assumed control of all matters educational. After struggling on for some years the ship's colours were, on 11 July 1974, finally laid up in Liverpool cathedral and the establishment was

The third and last *Warspite*, the old cruiser *Hermione*, moored off Grays in the 1930s.

closed. The closure of the *Conway* was, as with many of the training ships, a direct result of the demise of the British merchant fleet.

When the Shaftesbury Society replaced the *Arethusa* with the *Peking* in 1933, they retained the old ship's figurehead, putting it on display on the riverbank at Upnor. The figurehead is still there, in the grounds of what is now known as the *Arethusa* Venture Centre.

The *Peking*, renamed *Arethusa*, continued to train boys for the Royal and Merchant Navies until 1975. Then, when it was realised that the ship was uneconomical to repair and maintain, and with almost no demand for trained sailors any more, she was sold off to the South Street Seaport Museum in New York. Returned to her 1911 condition and under her original name, she remains a central exhibit in the floating museum.

The Shaftesbury Society was forced to reassess its role and its services in the wake of an expanding local government childcare system following the 1969 Children and Young Persons Act. As a result, the old *Arethusa* shore base at Upnor was redeveloped as an adventure education centre offering short breaks to children, wherever possible to those who would otherwise never have such an opportunity. An offshore cruising ketch provided experience of sailing and life afloat while the Arethusa Venture Centre offered such activities as rock climbing and swimming. These days the society continues its work but it is a far cry from the halcyon days of the old *Arethusa* and *Chichester*.

The Marine Society, the oldest marine charity in the world, is also still in existence, although its training ships have long been consigned to memory. Following the *Warspite* fire of 1918 the boys still in the early stages of their training (about 150 of them) were dispersed, ships such as the *President*, *Impregnable* and *Exmouth* all taking large numbers so that they could continue with their courses. For a short period the society also used Tilbury Hotel as a base before the Admiralty finally agreed to loan them the cruiser *Hermione*. Converted and renamed *Warspite* she lay in the Thames, training boys for the foc'sle – the society was always clear that it was up to the individual boy to progress himself once he had joined up – until war broke out in 1939.

The committee decided, reluctantly, that they could not justify retaining a large number of young boys on board the *Warspite* during wartime. Thirty of the boys had already joined the Royal and Merchant Navies, the rest were sent home to await their 'call up' in due course. In 1940 the *Warspite* was sold to help the government's drive for scrap metal.[134]

Due to the decline in the British Merchant Marine, there was to be no new *Warspite* in the post-war days, although some limited form of training was offered on small sea-going vessels. In 1976 the society merged with Incorporated Thames Nautical Training College – the old *Worcester*. The society now offers a wide range of services including the provision of Seafarers' Libraries and the running of the Worcester Scholarships.

By the late 1970s there was virtually no sea training on offer in the country – at least not in the same way as the wooden walls once provided it. The Royal Navy had already rationalised its training facilities and those schools that survived – places like Christ's College or the J. A. Gibbs Home (renamed Headlands in the years after the Second World War) – had radically altered their range of services. It was the end of a system, but more than that, it was the end of a remarkable and distinguished period of British maritime history.

Conclusion

The enormous network of training ships and schools created in Britain during the nineteenth century came about as a direct result of need. Firstly, as an island nation, there was the need to provide a trained and ready body of sailors for the Merchant and, occasionally, the Royal Navies. Secondly, society had a need to control delinquent, semi-delinquent and vagrant children so that they would not become an unhealthy or unmanageable burden. The hard discipline of the training ships would provide exactly that.

To the Victorian and Edwardian merchant capitalists – and, indeed, to educationalists – it was a matter of economics. If Britain did not have an effective and efficient Merchant Marine then the country would have to buy in such services from foreign powers – hugely expensive and not really controllable. The burden of crime and poor relief on the taxpayer was equally as unpalatable. The pragmatic approach was, ultimately, the only way to go.

However, if economics brought the schools into existence, economics also brought about their downfall. Sailing ships needed huge numbers of men to work them, to furl and unfurl the sails, to winch in the anchor, to simply man the ships. Once steam power succeeded sail, the need for such large numbers of sailors was drastically reduced.

There was a depression in maritime trades after both the First and Second World Wars. After 1945, although there were several false dawns, the decline was terminal. As Britain's merchant fleet dwindled, as air transport began to bite into the traditional sea-borne routes, as foreign shipping lines began to offer cheaper services, the need for trained sailors went with it. Even the Royal Navy with its streamlined vessels, its high-tech facilities and its altered role in world affairs, now requires fewer sailors than ever.

Not always hugely successful, the training ships were a remarkable feature of British maritime and coastal life for well over a hundred years. To many people they symbolised the grandeur and the glory of the past, being seen as a direct link to Nelson's wooden walls. It was inevitable that, as time ravaged their hulls and decks, the old ships would eventually disappear. What no one could foresee was the rapid decline and death of the British Merchant Marine, so when the schools

Duty's Call, boys from the *Mars* man the yards of the tender *Francis Mollison*.

The *Cornwall* band – proud and happy, boys being given a purpose in life.

closed it often came as a shock, leaving people with nostalgic memories and very little else.

The old training ships may have gone, but their memories remain; memories and stories that are as much a part of British maritime life as tales about the defeat of the Armada and Nelson's message at Trafalgar. Truly, we shall not see their like again.

Notes

1. *Lloyd's List*, 23 (January 1918).
2. Phil Carradice, article in *Bygone Kent*, vol. 18, no. 10 (October 1997).
3. Quoted in John Masefield, *The Conway* (London, Heinemann, 1933), p.59.
4. Michael Paterson, *Life in Victorian Britain* (London, Constable & Robinson, 2008), p.127.
5. Winston Churchill, *The World Crisis* (London, Four Square Books, undated), p.75.
6. E. C. Millington, *Seamen in the Making* (London, J. D. Potter, 1935), p.25.
7. Clement Jones, *Sea Trading & Training* (London, Arnold, 1936), p.75.
8. Quoted in *The Christ's Hospital Book* (London, Hamish Hamilton, 1953), p.66.
9. Ibid., p.67.
10. Phil Carradice, article in *Picture Postcard Monthly*, July 1992.
11. H. D. Turner, *The Cradle of the Navy* (York, Sevins Ltd, 1990), p.44.
12. Phil Carradice, article in *Picture Postcard Monthly*.
13. Turner, *The Cradle of the Navy*, p.44.
14. Donald G. Bovill, 'The Education of Boys for the Mercantile Marine' in *The History of Education Society Bulletin*, no. 47 (Spring 1991), 11.
15. Ibid., 15.
16. Ibid., 15.
17. The Newcastle Commission, *The State of Popular Education in England*, HMSO, vol. III, p.278.
18. James Stephen Taylor, *Jonas Hanway* (London, Scolar Press, 1985), p.185.
19. M. R. Penwarden, 'Juvenile Delinquency in Victorian London' (unpublished MSc thesis, Swansea, 1976), p.6.
20. Jo Manton, *Mary Carpenter and the Children of the Streets* (London, Heinemann, 1976), p.4.
21. J. S. Hurt, *Outside the Mainstream* (London, Batsford, 1988), p.66.
22. M. R. Day, 'A Child's Punishment for a Child's Crime' (unpublished PhD thesis, London, 1981), p.21.

23. Mary Carpenter, *Reformatory Schools for the Children of the Perishing and Dangerous Classes* (London, Gilpin, 1851), VI.

24. Act 17 & 18 Vict. ch. 86

25. 25th Report of Inspector of Reformatory and Industrial Schools.

26. Phil Carradice, article in *Sea Breezes*, vol. 66, no. 561, 717-727.

27. 9th Report of Inspector of Reformatory and Industrial Schools, 1866.

28. James P. Organ, *Hints on the Educational, Moral & Industrial Training of the Inmates of our Reformatories and Workhouses* (privately printed, 1860), p.57.

29. House of Commons Parliamentary Papers, vol. LXVIII, 1896, pp.482-577

30. Minutes of the Liverpool Reformatory Association, quoted in Joan Rimmer, *Yesterday's Naughty Children* (Manchester, Richardson, 1986), p.16.

31. Inspection Report on TS *Clarence*, 2 May 1889.

32. 25th Report of Inspector of Reformatory and Industrial Schools, 1882.

33. Henry Rogers, Report 1891, HO45/9822, B8262 E

34. 1st Report of Inspector of Reformatory and Industrial Schools, 1857.

35. 2nd Report of Inspector of Reformatory and Industrial Schools, 1858.

36. Inspection Report on *Akbar* and *Clarence*, May 1889.

37. Ibid.

38. Act for Amending and Consolidating the Law Relating to Industrial Schools, 24 & 25 Vict. ch. III.

39. The Newcastle Commission, p.160.

40. Commission on Manning the Navy, 1858, quoted in J. D. Potter, *Seamen in the Making.*

41. Letter, in possession of author.

42. Mary Carpenter, letter in *Cardiff and Merthyr Guardian*, 21 April 1860.

43. Report of Reformatory School Inspectors, quoted in Report to the *Havannah* Committee, 1866.

44. Report of Reformatory and Industrial School Inspectors, 1896.

45. Reports of *Havannah* School Committee, 1858 to 1903.

46. Ian David Cowan, *Industrial Schools and Training Ships, with Special Reference to the Humber Training Ship Southampton* (unpublished MEd. thesis, Hull, 1980), p.11.

47. Report of Inspector of Reformatory and Industrial Schools, 1889, quoted in Cowan, *Industrial Schools and Training Ships.*

48. Report of the *Mars* Committee, 1871, quoted in Cowan.

49. Hansard, HC Deb 21st March 1898, vol. 55, cc 389-90.

50. Report of Inspector of Reformatory and Industrial Schools, 1889.

51. Admiral Field, Notice of Motion, 1895.

52. Report of Henry Rogers to Home Office, HO45/9822 B8262 E

53. Report of Departmental Committee on Reformatory and Industrial Schools, HMSO, 1913.

54. Report of the Commissioners on Manning the Navy, 3rd September to 19th April 1859, vol. VI, XV.

55. Cowan, *Industrial Schools and Training Ships*, p.61.

56. Edwin Hodder, *The Life and Work of the 7ᵗʰ Earl of Shaftesbury* (London, Cassell, 1886).

57. Diary of Earl of Shaftesbury, quoted in Hodder.

58. Jack Lacey, article in *Bygone Kent*, vol. 9, no. 9, 507.

59. Ronald Morris, *The Captain's Lady* (London, Chatto and Windus, 1985), p.87.

60. Ibid., p.88.

61. Ibid., p.169.

62. Ibid., pp.17 – 18.

63. Alexander Gammie, *A Romance of Faith* (London, Pickering and Inglis Ltd), p.122.

64. Brian D. Price, 'Dancing to the Band of the Foudroyant' in *The Western Telegraph*, 22 July 1987.

65. Quoted in *The Conway*.

66. John Masefield, quoted in *The Conway*, p.3.

67. Ibid., p.64.

68. Ibid., p.31.

69. Quoted in Masefield, *The Conway*, p.55.

70. Frederick H. Stafford, *The History of the Worcester* (London, Frederick Warne & Co., 1929), p.17.

71. Ibid., p.22.

72. Admiral Count Togo, 29ᵗʰ June 1911, quoted in Stafford, *The History of the Worcester*.

73. Clement Jones, *Sea Trading and Sea Training* (London, Arnold, 1936), p.119.

74. Ibid., p.131.

75. Guy N. Pocock, *The Watts Naval Training School* (London, Barnardo's, 1932).

76. June Rose, *For the Sake of the Children* (London, Futura, 1987), p.156.

77. Barnardo Council Minute, quoted in *For the Sake of the Children*.

78. Rose, *For the Sake of the Children*, p.158.

79. Phil Carradice, *A History of Headlands School* (unpublished MEd. thesis, Cardiff, 1989), p.62.

80. Quoted in Carradice, *A History of Headlands School*, p.60.

81. J. A. Gibbs Home Log Book, quoted in Carradice, *A History of Headlands School*, pp.132-133.

82. Quoted in Carradice, *A History of Headlands School*, p.63.

83. Quoted in Carradice, *A History of Headlands School*, p.56.

84. Jones, *Sea Trading and Sea Training*, p.79.

85. R. A. Fletcher, *A Guide to the Mercantile Marine* (London, Pitman & Sons, undated), p.38.

86. Jones, *Sea Trading and Sea Training*, p.108.

87. Phil Carradice, *A Town in Conflict* (Penarth, Penarth Press, 2006), p.105.

88. Roy Derham, *Vindicatrix* (Buckingham, Baron Birch, 1993), p.72.

89. Ibid., p.89.
90. Report of the Commissioners on Manning the Navy, vol. VI, HMSO, VI.
91. John Winton, *Hurrah For the Life of a Sailor* (London, Michael Joseph, 1977), p.106.
92. Ibid., p.59.
93. Hansard HC 12th January 1894, vol. 20, c1447
94. Ibid.
95. John Douglas, *HMS Ganges: Roll on my Dozen* (Kineton, Roundwood Press, 1978), p.37.
96. Ibid., p.55.
97. Captain S. W. C. Pack, *Britannia at Dartmouth* (London, Alvin Redman, 1966), p.31.
98. Ibid., p.49-50.
99. Geoffrey Haskins, *The School That Jack Built* (Arcturus Press, 1999), p.3.
100. Ibid., p.8.
101. Article in *The Kentish Mercury*, 8 January 1876.
102. Carradice, article in *Bygone Kent*, October 1997, 576.
103. Article in *Liverpool Echo*, 17 January 1884, 4.
104. Article in *Liverpool Daily Post*, 18 January 1884, 5.
105. Article in *The Birkenhead News*, 2 February 1884, 5.
106. Article in *Liverpool Echo*, 26 July 1899, 3.
107. Rimmer, *Yesterday's Naughty Children*, p.43.
108. Brian Price, article in *Western Telegraph*, 22 July 1987.
109. John Cowell, 'The Wreck of HMS *Conway*' in *Picture Postcard Monthly*, no. 150, October 1991, 16.
110. Ibid., p.16.
111. Patricia O'Driscoll, article in *Archive*, vol. 2, no. 1, March 1995, 47.
112. Ibid., p.52.
113. Article in *John Bull*, Saturday 22 October 1910, 626.
114. Ibid., 626-627.
115. Julius Carlebach, *Caring for Children in Trouble* (London, Routledge and Kegan Paul, 1970), pp.78-86.
116. Rimmer, *Yesterday's Naughty Children*, p.28.
117. Hurt, *Outside the Mainstream*, p.80.
118. 5th Annual Report of the Clio, quoted in Emrys Wyn Roberts, 'The Clio' (MEd. thesis, Bangor, undated), p.25.
119. Cowan, *Industrial Schools and Training Ships*, p.39.
120. Letter from Captain Williams of the *Cornwall* to the Inspector of Reformatory and Industrial Schools, 30th June 1903. Document B212202, HO45/10413
121. Article in *Eastern Daily Press*, 14 November 1902.
122. Article in *Daily Mail*, 21 May 1903
123. Letter from Home Office Inspector, Document B19615, HO 45/10413
124. Bill Meilem, *The Division* (Panther, 1967), p.18.

125. Article in *The Times*, Wednesday 14 February 1906.
126. Report of Inspectors of Reformatory and Industrial Schools, June 1901, B19615
127. Robert K. Massie, *Dreadnought* (London, Pimlico, 1991), p.161.
128. Report on the Proceedings of the Fourth National Conference on Sea Training, 'Back to the Sea', HMSO, 21 October 1913, p.1.
129. Report of the Departmental Committee on Reformatory and Industrial Schools, 1913, p.98.
130. Rimmer, *Yesterday's Naughty Children*, pp.38-40.
131. Cowan, *Industrial Schools and Training Ships*, pp.69-70.
132. Turner, *The Cradle of the Navy*, p.130.
133. Ronald Morris, *The Captain's Lady*, pp.131-132.
134. Article in *The Liverpool Journal of Commerce*, 7 October 1939.

Bibliography

PRIMARY SOURCES

Reports

Hansard and Parliamentary Papers (Law Library, Cardiff University)

The Newcastle Commission, 1861

Report of Commissioners on Manning the Navy, 3rd September 1858 to 19th April 1859

Report of the Departmental Committee on Reformatory and Industrial Schools, 1913

Reports of the *Havannah* Committee, 1858 to 1903 (held at Cardiff Central Library)

Reports of the Inspector of Reformatory and Industrial Schools, 1857 to 1913 – all available at the Public Records Office, Kew – including letters from the various inspectors and ship captain superintendents/staff

Report of the Proceedings of the Fourth National Conference on Sea Training, 1913 ('Back to the Sea')

Newspapers

Birkenhead News

Cardiff and Merthyr Guardian

Daily Mail

Eastern Daily Press

John Bull

The Kentish Mercury

Liverpool Daily Post

Liverpool Echo

Liverpool Journal of Commerce

The Times

The Western Mail

The Western Telegraph

Magazines
Approved School Gazette
Archive
Bygone Kent
The City Press
Community Homes School Gazette
Highways and Hedges (NCH magazine)
History of Education Society Bulletin
Lloyd's List
Mariners Mirror
Maritime Wales
Picture Postcard Monthly
Sea Breezes
Social Work Today

Unpublished University Theses

Carradice, Phil, 'A History of Headlands School 1918 – 1986,' MEd, University of
    Wales College, Cardiff, 1989.
Cowan, Ian David, 'Industrial Schools and Training Ships, with Special Reference
    to the Humber Training Ship Southampton,' MEd, Hull, 1980.
Day, M. R., 'A Child's Punishment for a Child's Crime,' PhD, London, 1981.
Jordan, Anita Loosemore, 'The History and Development of the Education of the
    Delinquent, Mentally and Physically Handicapped and Pauper Child in Wales,
    from 1833 to 1933,' PhD, Wales, 1977.
Penwarden, M. R., 'Juvenile Delinquency in Victorian London,' MSc, University
    of Wales College, Swansea, 1980.
Roberts, Emrys Wyn, 'The Clio: A Study of the Functions of an Industrial Training
    Ship in North Wales,' MEd, Bangor, undated.
Rooke, Patrick John, 'Education in the Treatment of Young Offenders During the
    Nineteenth Century in England and Wales,' PhD, Bulmershe, 1985.

SECONDARY SOURCES

Benham, Hervey, *Last Stronghold of Sail* (London, Harrap, 1948)
Branch-Johnson, *The English Prison Hulks* (London, Christopher Johnson,
    1957)
Carlebach, Julius. *Caring for Children in Trouble* (London, Routledge and Kegan
    Paul, 1970)
Carpenter, Mary, *Reformatory Schools for the Children of the Perishing and
    Dangerous Classes* (London, Gilpin, 1851)
Carradice, Phil, *A Town in Conflict*, (Penarth, Penarth Press, 2006)
—, *Pembroke Dock: The Town Built to Build Ships* (Bedlinog, Accent Press,
    2006)
Chesney, Kellow, *The Victorian Underworld* (Devon, Readers Union, 1970)

Christ's Hospital, *The Christ's Hospital Book 1553-1953* (London, Hamish Hamilton, 1953)

Churchill, Winston, *The World Crisis* (London, Four Square Books, undated)

Derham, Roy, *Vindicatrix* (Buckingham, Baron Birch, 1993)

Douglas, John, *Roll on my Dozen* (Kineton, Roundwood Press, 1978)

Endacott, Andy, *Naval Heritage in the West*, vols I, II & III (Plymouth, privately printed, 1986-1988)

Fletcher, R. A., *A Guide to the Mercantile Marine* (London, Pitman & Sons, undated)

Gammie, Alexander, *A Romance of Faith* (London, Pickering & Inglis Ltd, undated)

Grove, Eric, *Great Battles of the Royal Navy* (Godalming, Colour Library Direct, 1998)

Haskins, Geoffrey, *The School That Jack Built* (Arcturus Press, 1999)

Hodder, Edwin, *The Life of the 7th Earl of Shaftesbury KG*, (London Cassell, 1886)

Hurt, J. S., *Outside the Mainstream* (London, Batsford, 1988)

James, Lawrence, *The Rise and Fall of the British Empire* (London, Abacus, 1998)

Jones, Clement, *Sea Trading and Sea Training* (London, Edward Arnold, 1936)

Manton, Jo, *Mary Carpenter and the Children of the Streets* (London, Heinemann, 1976)

Masefield, John, *The Conway* (London, Heinemann, 1933)

Massie, Robert K., *Dreadnought* (London, Pimlico, 1991)

Mayberry, Dr John, *I Saw Three Ships* (Lancashire, Silver Link Publishing, undated)

Meilem, Bill, *The Division* (London, Panther, 1967)

Millington, E. C., *Seamen in the Making* (London, Edward Arnold & Co, 1935)

Morris, Jan, *Fisher's Face* (London, Penguin, 1996)

Morris, Ronald, *The Captain's Lady* (London, Chatto and Windus, 1985)

Norman, F. M., *A History of HMS Havannah School Ship, Cardiff* (Cardiff, Western Mail Ltd, 1904)

Organ, James P., *Hints on the Educational, Moral and Industrial Training of the Inmates of our Reformatories and Workhouses* (Dublin, privately printed, 1860)

Pack, Captain S. W. C., *Britannia at Dartmouth*, (London, Alvin Redman, 1966)

Paterson, Michael, *Life in Victorian Britain* (London, Constable and Robinson, 2008)

Pocock, Guy, *The Watts Naval Training School* (London, Barnardos, 1932)

Rimmer, Joan, *Yesterday's Naughty Children* (Manchester, Richardson, 1986)

Rose, June, *For the Sake of the Children* (London, Futura, 1987)

Stafford, Frederick, *The History of the Worcester* (London, Warne & Co, 1929)

Taylor, James Stephen, *Jonas Hanway* (London, Scolar Press, 1985)

Thomas, David, *Royal Admirals* (London, Andre Deutsch, 1982)

Turner, H. D. *The Cradle of the Navy* (York, Sevins Ltd, 1990)

Watkins, Frederick, *Ship Reformatories and Industrial Schools* (privately printed, 1858)

Watts, Anthony J., *A Pictorial History of the Royal Navy*, vol. II (London, Ian Allen, 1971)

Wilson, A. N., *The Victorians* (London, Hutchinson, 2002)

Winton, John, *Hurrah for the Life of a Sailor* (London, Michael Joseph, 1977)

N.B. For readers who enjoy novels there are two full-length stories – fictional but clearly based on true events – that use nautical schools as their setting. *The Division* by Bill Meilem (Panther) is set in the 1940s/1950s, in an approved school for delinquent boys, a school that has clear nautical connections. *The Bosun's Secret* by Phil Carradice (Pont Books, Gomer Press) is set on board the Cardiff training ship *Havannah* in 1870 and is concerned with the life of one boy over a six-month period on the vessel. Both books give a graphic account of what life was really like in the schools, albeit at different periods in time.

Acknowledgements

Grateful thanks to:
The staff of the Public Records Office, Kew
The staff of Cardiff Central Library
The staff of the Action for Children (formerly NCH) and Barnardo's Libraries
The staff of the Law Library, Cardiff University

Staff at the *Indefatigable* and *Wellesley* Schools, now closed, but which, when originally contacted, were still open and running

All the countless individuals who, over the years, have sent me information and photographs – in particular thanks to Miss Pat O'Driscoll for her knowledge and continued encouragement.

Most of the photographs in the book come from the author's personal collection but particular thanks must be given to the following individuals and organisations for the loan of certain images: Stephen Rowson, Jim O'Neil, Museum of London/PLA Collection, Museum in Docklands Project, Commander Johnson of Heswall School and the National Nautical School, Portishead.

Above all, and as always, huge thanks to Trudy for her patience and encouragement during the writing of this book.

Also from Amberley Publishing

*THE ILLUSTRATED
SINKING OF THE TITANIC*

L T MYERS

PRICE: £17.99

ISBN: 978 1 84868 053 1

SIZE: 248 X 172MM

Fully illustrated and comprehensive
account of the ship's final days.

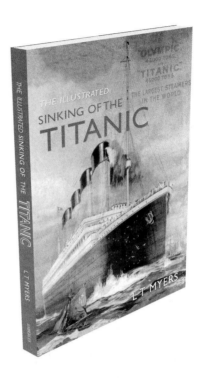

*THE ILLUSTRATED
TRUTH ABOUT THE TITANIC*

ARCHIBALD GRACIE

PRICE: £17.99

ISBN: 978-1-84868-093-7

SIZE: 248 X 172MM

The first fully illustrated version of
Archibald Gracie's memoir Titanic
Survivor.

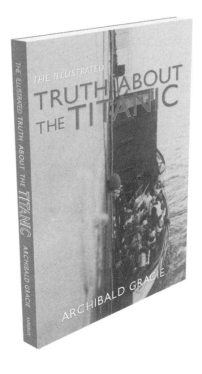

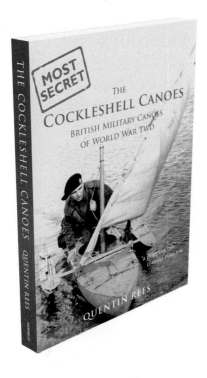

THE COCKLESHELL CANOES

QUENTIN REES

PRICE: £19.99

ISBN: 978 1 84868 065 4

SIZE: 248 X 172MM

The gripping story of the development of the Cockleshell Canoes.

CUNARDS THREE QUEENS
A CELEBRATION

WILLIAM H MILLER

PRICE: £25

ISBN: 978-1-84868-364-8

SIZE: 246 X 248MM

A profusely illustrated history of the greatest Cunard Queens.